Library of Shakespearean Biography and Criticism

I. PRIMARY REFERENCE WORKS ON SHAKESPEARE

II. CRITICISM AND INTERPRETATION

    A. Textual Treatises, Commentaries
    B. Treatment of Special Subjects
    C. Dramatic and Literary Art in Shakespeare

III. SHAKESPEARE AND HIS TIME

    A. General Treatises. Biography
    B. The Age of Shakespeare
    C. Authorship

Series II, Part C

SHAKESPEARE'S HISTORIES
AT STRATFORD, 1951

Design for the permanent set by Tanya Moiseiwitsch.

Library of Shakespearean Biography and Criticism

SHAKESPEARE'S HISTORIES
AT STRATFORD
1951

by
JOHN DOVER WILSON
and
THOMAS C. WORSLEY

Photographs by
ANGUS McBEAN

BOOKS FOR LIBRARIES PRESS
FREEPORT, NEW YORK

First published in 1952
All Rights Reserved

Reprinted 1970 by arrangement with the original publishers,
Theatre Arts Books, New York

INTERNATIONAL STANDARD BOOK NUMBER:
0-8369-5515-3

LIBRARY OF CONGRESS CATALOG CARD NUMBER:
73-128895

PRINTED IN THE UNITED STATES OF AMERICA

ACKNOWLEDGEMENTS

THE publishers express their thanks to the following for their permission to quote: Mr. Brian Harvey and the editor of the *Birmingham Gazette;* the editor of *The Birmingham Mail;* Mr. T. C. Kemp and the editor of *The Birmingham Post;* Mr. Cecil Wilson and the editor of the *Daily Mail;* Mr. W. A. Darlington and the editor of *The Daily Telegraph;* Mr. T. A. Jackson and the editor of the *Daily Worker;* the editor of *The Manchester Guardian;* the editor of *The New Statesman and Nation;* Mr. Alan Dent and the editor of the *News Chronicle;* Mr. Ivor Brown and the editor of *The Observer;* Mr. Eric Keown and the proprietors of *Punch;* Mr. J. C. Trewin and the editor of *The Sketch;* Mr. Peter Fleming and the editor of *The Spectator;* Mr. Harold Hobson, Mr. J. W. Lambert, and the editor of the *Sunday Times;* Mr. Robert Speaight and the editor of *The Tablet;* Mr. Philip Hope-Wallace and the editor of *Time and Tide;* the editor of *The Times;* Mr. Richard Findlater and the editor of *Tribune;* the editor of *Truth;* Miss Siriol Hugh Jones and the editor of *Vogue.*

They gratefully acknowledge the kindness of the editor of " The Year's Work in the Theatre 1950-51," published for the British Council by Messrs. Longmans, Green and Co., for lending them the colour blocks of Miss Moiseiwitsch's set, which appears as a frontispiece to this volume.

They also acknowledge with thanks the help they have received from Mr. George Hume, general manager of the Shakespeare Memorial Theatre, and Mr. John Goodwin, its press representative.

CONTENTS

FOREWORD

THE RESOURCES of the Shakespeare Memorial Theatre and the occasion of the Festival of Britain combined in 1951 to bring about a rare theatrical phenomenon — the performance in sequence of Shakespeare's four History Plays, *Richard II, Henry IV* Parts I and II, and *Henry V.* Records show that these plays were performed as a cycle by Sir Frank Benson's company at Stratford in 1905; otherwise I cannot ascertain that they have been played in this country as a cycle since Shakespeare's day.

In approaching our tasks the producers — Michael Redgrave, John Kidd and myself, together with our designer Tanya Moiseiwitsch — never doubted but that the plays were written as one great tetralogy, though the contents and difference in style of *Richard II* made us think that Shakespeare intended that play rather as a prologue to the other three. We well knew that each play was strong enough to stand theatrically on its own feet, and that economic necessity for many years had forced them to do so; but the more we studied the more we felt that this practice of presenting the plays singly had only resulted in their distortion, and that their full power and meaning only became apparent when treated as a whole. It was not only that many of the characters lived and developed through several of the plays; it was not only that literary and dramatic echoes reverberated backwards and forwards through the text of all four; it was because what appeared to be puzzling psychological inconsistencies when the plays were treated singly disappeared when they were considered as a whole, and became clear as purposeful and masterly writing.

The plays have come to be thought of as separate entities since the economic and organizational difficulties in the way of presenting the cycle as a whole are so formidable. Thus *Richard II* has tended to become only a vehicle for a great star playing Richard — and a wonderful vehicle it is too — but in the process the great role of Bolingbroke emerges only as a moderate supporting part, and the political implications — so essential if the next plays are to be understood — go for next to nothing. In *Henry IV* Part I, Hotspur's part is far more rewarding than Hal's, so Hotspur has always been the choice of the star, who naturally plays it for all the sympathy he can get. But in doing this he distorts the true dramatic value of the play, for Shakespeare clearly means our sympathies to be with Hal more than with Hotspur. Hotspur is a hero, but he is a hero *manqué*, and if one of the two must fall at Shrewsbury then Shakespeare has been urging us throughout the play to choose Hal as the survivor. Falstaff himself is a tremendous star-vehicle, and few stars will risk their chances of success by showing the unsympathetic, even repellent side of his character: how can they when the commercial success of Part II (presented singly) must depend on Falstaff's popularity? But Shakespeare makes no bones about it: his Falstaff is irresistibly loveable — but he is also frankly vicious. Finally, there is Hal — usually so shorn and mangled in both parts of *Henry IV* that he is unrecognizable when he emerges into *Henry V*, and so misrepresented as the frank, boon companion of Falstaff that we can only feel nauseated by his priggish renunciation of his friend. But again the real key to that relationship is in the text itself: in his first soliloquy Hal shows us with what reserve he treats his tavern friends, and begins to prepare us for the inevitability of that final renunciation. Falstaff, though he certainly has an eye to the main chance, truly loves the boy and shows it. Hal never declares his affection for Falstaff: on the contrary, he is outspoken — and misunderstood in his outspokenness — in condemnation of the fat knight.

In short, it seemed to us that the great epic theme of the Histories had become obscured through years of presenting the plays singly, and many false interpretations had grown up, and come to be accepted, through star actors giving almost too persuasive and dominant performances of parts which the author intended to be by no means so sympathetic. Successful

viii

Opposite. " In the devotion of a subject's love . .
Come I appellant to this princely presence."
The prologue to the Cycle. Bolingbroke lays before the
King the quarrel with Mowbray which leads to his banishment.

theatrical practice over a great number of years had stealthily built a mountain of misrepresentation and surrounded it with a fog of ignorance. This was the producers' belief as we worked on the plays, and our purpose in presenting the History Cycle was to rediscover and try to reveal the author's true intentions.

The next greatest problem was to devise a single setting which could serve all four plays, for to have invented different settings for each play would have destroyed that very unity for which we were striving, that unity which Shakespeare's own Globe preserved so well. The set had to be capable of embracing court and tavern, shire and city, indoor and out-of-door; it had to be the lists at Coventry and the quay-side at Southampton; it had to house the rebels in their barn before the battle of Shrewsbury, and the dying Bolingbroke in the Jerusalem chamber; and, since this list must have an end, it had to suggest the " wooden O " of *Henry V.* All of these problems — at any rate to my mind and to those of my co-producers — Miss Moiseiwitsch solved triumphantly. Of course some scenes and certain plays were better served than others, but in our opinion her set was a masterpiece of imaginative yet disciplined stage-design.

Now actors — and by ' actors ' I mean producers as well — have a rewarding life, for, unlike most other artists, they can witness at first hand the impact of their work: no actor who can move an audience to horror, or laughter, or pity, need doubt that he has exerted some influence in his own lifetime. And with this they should be content. But being artists, and human, they wish to eat their cake, have it, and even be assured that they will leave behind a few posthumous crumbs: they would like to think that their performances could be purchased for the nation and fill a space or two in the Tate Gallery, or endure for posterity in a uniform edition, handsomely bound, the copyright jealously guarded by a fashionable publishing house. But no: when the curtain falls their performance can live only a human span in the failing memories of their

Opposite. " We are amazed and thus long have we stood
To watch the fearful bending of thy knee."
Bolingbroke returned from exile waits (left) while Northumberland carries his allegiance to Richard at Flint Castle.

audience, and for immortality they must depend on the temper, taste and talent of the dramatic critic.

"For pity's sake!" the critic will now cry "Do not thrust such a responsibility on me. Remember I am a journalist, and fallacious. Every year I am allotted less space, and often my notice must be composed — and telephoned to my paper — within an hour of curtain-fall on the first, worst, night. If you actors have got to suffer from immortal longings, do not make me their custodian. I am flattered, but I decline the honour."

I cannot help it: that is the situation. And that is why, no matter how much they pretend to ignore the professional criticisms of their work, actors will always hope for recognition from this most articulate section of their public; they will rejoice when their aims are understood, and they will be driven to cold exasperation when they are treated with ignorance or facetiousness.

All of which explains why I am particularly happy, and honoured, to have been asked to write a foreword to this book, for though the production and performance of the cycle was a labour of great love it was also a great labour, and all of us who took part in it must welcome a book which guarantees that labour some degree of permanence — for it may be many years again before the cycle is produced.

Those who saw the productions at Stratford no doubt made up their own minds as to how far we failed or succeeded in our aims ; those who did not see them can read in this book the observations of two most perceptive minds. Professor Dover Wilson is world-famous both for his humanity and his scholarship; Mr. Worsley is held by all who work in the theatre to be one of the most sensitive and discerning of our younger dramatic critics. I welcome the publication of this book in that it rightly binds together the functions of three professions — those of actor, scholar and critic — all of them essential to vital work in the theatre.

ANTHONY QUAYLE

Stratford-upon-Avon,
April, 1952.

SHAKESPEARE
AND ENGLISH HISTORY
AS THE ELIZABETHANS
UNDERSTOOD IT

by

J. DOVER WILSON

IF THE spirit of Shakespeare, wearying a little of "wit combats" with Aeschylus and Euripides, Racine and Molière, has risen now and again during the past three centuries from his couch of flowers in Elysium to revisit the glimpses of the moon, he must have wondered which of his official interpreters, the actor or the scholar, was misinterpreting him most. Each has much indeed of illumination and understanding to give, but the trouble is that either without guidance from the other is liable to grievous error. The attitude of the theatre, for instance, during the 18th century was the negation of scholarship. Actors and producers had little regard to Shakespeare's purposes and none for his text, so that *King Lear* was usually given a happy ending, supplied with other "improvements" by Nahum Tate ; and the plays generally were treated as so many lengths of raw material to be cut up and reshaped in performance according to the whim of the company concerned. It is not therefore surprising that Dr. Johnson should have expressed contempt for the acting profession, despite the fact that Garrick, his friend and fellow townsman, was then its leading light, or that Charles Lamb in the next generation declared that to put *King Lear* on the stage was a sacrilegious absurdity. A little later still, no doubt, actors began to pay more respect to

1

textual fidelity, but new modes of distortion came into fashion. Kean, Irving, and Beerbohm Tree, all great actors in different ways and devoted Shakespearians, delighted to smother the plays in elaborate scenery, extraneous pageantry, and even at times sheer pantomime. Well do I remember a performance of *A Midsummer Night's Dream* at His Majesty's Theatre, to which all London flocked and sat spellbound at the spectacle of *real* rabbits on the stage, which was enclosed in visible wire-netting to prevent them escaping into the auditorium ; and one of *Richard II* at the same theatre which was obviously designed to rival Wilson Barrett's *Sign of the Cross*. Nor can it be denied that even some of our modern producers, more anxious to exhibit their own brilliance than Shakespeare's masterpieces in their integrity, will " set on some quantity of barren spectators " to gape at their antics, " though in the mean time some necessary question of the play be then to be considered." And a little scholarship, of the wrong kind, may prove even more dangerous than scholarship flouted, as when not long ago a platinum blonde Cleopatra appeared on the boards of the Stratford Memorial Theatre, in defiance of Shakespeare's references to her " tawny front," because the distinguished producer happened to have discovered from the pages of *The Cambridge Ancient History* that she had probably been in fact a Greek, or at least a Macedonian, princess !

But if Shakespeare's fellows, the actor and producer, are too prone to think of his works as merely theatre-pieces for the display of their own persons or notions, the Shakespearian scholar and critic are often guilty of a far worse error, that of thinking of them as merely books, an error which is itself the fruitful parent of many other errors. One of the prevailing fallacies of XIXth century Shakespearian criticism, for example, may be described as taking things out of their context : the critic treated a play as history and considered the characters

2

Opposite. " Here, cousin, seize the crown . . .
On this side my hand and on that side yours."
Richard abdicates to Bolingbroke.

in isolation, as if they were historical persons, instead of being aspects or points of reference in a single harmonious work of dramatic art ; or he adopted the omniscient attitude of science and arrived at his critical conclusions on the basis of evidence picked from any scene or episode, and in any order. *Hamlet* the play and Hamlet the character have been peculiarly subject to this sort of mishandling ; not the least flagrant example of it is Senor de Madariaga's recent book, which discovers the Prince of Denmark to be a Borgian paranoiac by ignoring all we are told about him in Act I. Every actor knows, that the context for a character is the drama in which he appears, the whole drama, and nothing but the drama ; that apart from the play, apart from his actions, from what he tells us about himself and what the other characters tell us about him, there is no Hamlet. And yet how much paper and ink have been wasted on speculation about his boyhood, his college days at Wittenberg, or his relations with Ophelia before the play begins, to say nothing of his complexes acquired in infancy. More-over, to understand him or any other character as his creator meant us to understand him, we must experience him in the order he is revealed to us ; another point which the actor never thinks of questioning, since he is bound of necessity to follow the play through from the first scene to the last.

Nor in some cases is it enough to watch a character for five acts before framing a judgement upon him. Two of Shake-speare's greatest characters are leading figures in a whole series of plays and may be seriously misunderstood when con-sidered within the framework, or from the point of view, of one play alone. I have in mind of course Henry of Monmouth and Sir John Falstaff, the first of whom has been almost universally judged (and condemned) by critics on the strength of his soliloquy in Act I Scene 2 of *Henry IV* Part I and of his action at the end of Part II, with hardly any regard to the

3

Opposite. " Great King, within this coffin I present Thy buried fear . . ." Bolingbroke, now Henry IV, faced with the crime that is to haunt him and his son all their reigns.

dramatist's presentation of him between these points, or as the victor of Agincourt in *Henry V*. Similarly the fat knight has been viewed and appraised almost entirely from the standpoint of Part I, one might even say of the Boar's Head scene of Part I, while what Bradley admits to be " the repellent traits " revealed in Part II have been overlooked or explained away. But in the theatre " the action lies in his true nature." There one cannot pick and choose but must sit and watch. And when a trilogy is in question one must sit and watch the whole series before one has any right to frame final conclusions about its characters.

It is for that reason, if for no other, that the Festival Season at Stratford-upon-Avon in 1951 opened a new chapter in our understanding and appreciation of Shakespeare, inasmuch as it allowed us to experience as spectators — for the first time since Benson's production in 1905[1] —all three Henry V plays, together with their tragic prelude of *Richard II*, and to experience them in their proper order. The season gave us much to be thankful for : superb acting, and honest-to-Shakespeare productions, based upon a prolonged and painstaking study of the Master's purposes and effects, which were in my judgement almost always justly interpreted. But what distinguished it above everything was its fresh revelation, surprising to many and even baffling to some, of Shakespeare's art, in particular of his art as a historian. And though it would be going too far, I think, to suppose that he planned the four plays from the beginning as one historical masterpiece in serial parts, like Hardy's *Dynasts*, their serial presentation on the stage emphasises the links he added to give them a measure of unity and coherence, links which are inevitably overlooked when they are given separate performances. As to character, I am bold to say that no one who witnessed with proper under-

[1] At Stratford. See Foreword, p. vii.

standing the four performances at Stratford will ever again be able to think of Falstaff and his royal partner, whether as Prince Hal or King Henry V, in the way Hazlitt and Swinburne, Bradley and Masefield, had taught us to think of them. For one thing, the discovery of the youthfulness of the victor of Agincourt took one's breath away; and yet it was perfectly right according to both history and Shakespeare. To credit mean and caddish actions, as the critics do, to this young and ardent knight, whom Shakespeare himself[2] calls the "mirror of all Christian kings" and "Star of England," would have been stupid. One critic at any rate left Stratford with a feeling of profound gratitude to Anthony Quayle and Michael Redgrave for what he had learnt; and, when he was asked for a contribution to this commemorative volume, compliance was but a slight acknowledgment of a large debt, while in the topic assigned to him he saw opportunity for scholarship, so far as he could command it, to supplement the findings of the stage.

In a sense Shakespeare was writing history plays for most of his career. For if you add to the ten plays on English history, the Roman histories *Julius Caesar*, *Antony and Cleopatra*, and *Coriolanus*, the British histories, *King Lear* and *Cymbeline*, and that great Scottish history *Macbeth*, you get a total of sixteen out of the thirty-six plays in the canon. But in grouping the English plays together, and labelling them " Histories " to distinguish them from the groups of " Comedies " and " Tragedies " which flank them on either side in the First Folio, the editors of that volume rightly marked them out as belonging to a special genre of their own. One has indeed only to compare *King Lear* with *Richard II*, both mainly devoted to the exhibition of a single character, developing under the stress of disaster from the intemperance of a tyrant

---

[2] For what the Chorus says is the dramatist's own opinion.

5

to something approaching the sanctity of martyrdom, to see that while the first is of course a tragedy of the highest order, the second is something different, which we must call a tragical "history." And the chief difference is not, as is often implied, that the structure of *Richard II* is looser than that of *King Lear* because the dramatist was not free to depart far from the "facts" presented by the chronicler. For though that is of course an important distinction, there is another more fundamental one, *viz.*, that in all ten English Histories both dramatist and audience are less concerned with the career and fortunes of the principal characters than with—

The sanity and health of this whole state

of England. In other words, their characters are seen and appraised in relation to a political background and political issues which were still actual for Elizabethan spectators, whereas in pure tragedy the background and issues are eternal. To understand Shakespeare's English histories to the full, therefore, one must know something of what history in general meant to his contemporaries and why they were interested in the periods he selected.

At that date history proper was of recent origin, or rather a recent discovery, since like other types of modern literature it began at the renaissance ; that is to say, it was the product on the one hand of the recovery of the classics, especially of the classical historians, and on the other of the rise of nation states, each eager to assert its independence of the loose con-federation we call medieval Christendom. Chronicles in the middle ages had been written by monks in monkish Latin to the glory of God ; and recorded the events of the past, from the creation downwards, as seen, or imagined, from within the walls of the monastery. Renaissance history was written by humanist scholars, at first in Latin of a Ciceronian vintage and later in the vernacular, and recorded the past of the writer's country or city-state, native or adopted, to the glory of the ruling house. It follows that Tudor history was entirely, even superstitiously, monarchical, and that its principal theme was the origin and glorification of the Tudor dynasty. In a word, it was an instrument of state propaganda, from which one must not expect an impartial treatment of the Yorkists whom Henry VII crushed; or of the old religion, once the Tudors had definitely thrown in their lot with the reformers. Let us not, however, flatter ourselves in this respect. The historians of every age are discovered to be propagandists by their successors in the next, and when thirty years ago I heard Austen Chamberlain (of all people !) speak of " the wealth of Whig tradition that lies behind the historical writings of Dr. Trevelyan," I realised that history as I had been taught it in my youth was due for the re-dressing upon which its modern practitioners are now busy. Moreover, the Tudor historians had a very plausible case, even if they did their best to make it seem more plausible than it was. But let Dr. Trevelyan, my own teacher at Cambridge, state it for us. After observing that " the keynote of Tudor government " was " king-worship, not despotism," he continues :— [3]

" Monarchs without an army at the centre or a paid bureaucracy in the country-side . . . could not compel their subjects by force — a population of five millions, many of whom had sword, bow, or bill hanging from the cottage rafters. The power of the Tudors . . . was not material but metaphysical. They appealed sometimes to the love and always to the loyalty and " free awe " of their subjects. In the century that begins with Sir Thomas More and ends with Shakespeare " the deputy elected by the Lord " walks girt with a sunlike majesty. In his (or her) presence rank, genius, religion veil their pride, or lay their heads resignedly upon the block, if the wrath of the Prince demands a sacrifice. English king-worship was the secret of a family and spirit of an age. It owed much to the political talents of the two Henries and Elizabeth, and yet more to the need for national leadership in a period of transition from the medieval to the modern world."

I know of no better introduction to a study of Shakespeare's history plays than this brilliant generalisation of our greatest living historian, which brings out the amazing fact that the strongest government this country has ever known had literally nothing to back it up — no standing army, no bureaucracy, no police except such as is represented by Dogberry and Verges in *Much Ado* — nothing but the adoration of the people. Trevelyan omits, however, one factor, an essential element of all true worship, gratitude. The Elizabethans could never be too grateful for the internal peace and social stability which the Tudors brought to England ; and one function of the Tudor historians was to express and to encourage this gratitude. Gratitude too was the mainspring of all Shakespeare's English histories, and the tacit assumption of the many thousand spectators who flocked to see them. Finally it was this gratitude which determined the choice of his material, the period of history reflected in nine out of the ten plays.

Every age has an epoch in the past of special interest to itself. To the Victorians, and I think still to the Edwardians, the section of our national history which seemed most significant was that which began with the struggle between the Stuarts and their parliaments and ended with the Whig compromise under William and Mary. The reason is obvious. Here our fathers and grandfathers found the origins of the political and social institutions under which they were proud to live, as Macaulay made clear when he began publishing about the time of the first Great Exhibition his *History of England* from the accession of James I to the death of William III. The corresponding period in the eyes of Tudor Englishmen lay two hundred years earlier, its culminating event being the Battle of Bosworth 1485 which ushered in their era no less decisively than the Revolution of 1688 did ours, while their representative historian was Edward Hall who in 1548, almost exactly four centuries before the appearance of Macaulay's *History*, published his *Union of the two noble and illustrious famelies of Lancastre and Yorke, beeying long in continual discension for the croune of this noble realme;* a book of genesis which was mainly concerned with an account of this "discension" and of the causes thereof. For Tudor Englishmen, like their successors in the 18th and 19th centuries, looked back to a great deliverance, a deliverance from the national curse of civil war ; from a time of chaos, insecurity, and bloodshed. They too rejoiced in special institutions which, though mostly swept away by the Puritan revolution, were themselves the product of a previous revolution, or rather of the compromise and national consolidation which followed that revolution. Their time of trouble was the Wars of the Roses and their saviour was the House of Tudor, which healed the breach by effecting a dynastic compromise ; Henry VIII being in Hall's words " the indubitable flower and very heir of both lineages." The constitution they rejoiced in was not a democracy, or a landed aristocracy with a party system and the paraphernalia of parliament graced with an ornamental monarchy, such as governed England during the eighteenth century, but a monarchy ruling through its own chosen council and through a nobility largely of its own creation ; a monarchy divinely ordained, absolute, unchallenged, and entirely popular.

The blessings of the Tudor settlement were indeed so patent and unquestionable to Shakespeare and his contemporaries that their only fear was of anything that might threaten the supremacy of the crown or the stability of the society they knew ; a social structure which like a pyramid of different ranks, ranged from the Prince at the apex through the various grades of greater nobles, lesser nobles, knights and gentry, merchants and yeomen farmers down to the broad base of the labouring poor. The most sensitive spot in the modern Englishman's political soul is personal liberty : let the executive touch that and in a few hours a storm may spring up that will shake the firmest government from its saddle. Equally touchy were the Elizabethans on the question of order. The Tudor settlement in the end made modern liberty possible. But liberty was a notion hardly comprehensible to Shakespeare and the only liberty the suppressed religious denominations of his time desired was a liberty to suppress those who differed from them. Read *Julius Caesar* through and you will nowhere find political liberty as we understand it even glanced at. And though I do not believe that Shakespeare had " order " on the brain to the extent which some recent writers would have us think, it is clear that he, like all his thoughtful contemporaries, regarded with horror any prospect of disturbing the harmony and balance of the body politic. He was particularly success-ful as a writer of crowd scenes ; and he always depicts his mobs as excitable, fickle, gullible, easily led astray by dem-agogues for their own ends. His mobs too are always London mobs, even in his Roman plays. "This is what you are like" he seems to say to his audience, " when you presume to dabble in politics."

The real danger to the state, however, lay not in mob rule — anyone could deal with that — but in a disputed succession. And when the 16th century Englishman looked back across the Flood to discover the origin of the troubles that had afflicted his grandparents and from which Henry VII had freed

10

Opposite. " Worcester, get thee gone, for I do see Danger and disobedience in thine eye." It is Bolingbroke's turn to face rebellion. Between Worcester and Harry Hotspur is Northumberland who has now changed sides.

them, he found it, quite correctly, in the reign of Richard II, when on account partly of Richard's insolence, incompetence, and folly, and partly of Bolingbroke's personal ambition, the Lord's anointed was deposed and murdered and his throne occupied by a usurper ; a " sin "[4] which set in motion all the evils that followed. It is no accident that Shakespeare's play on King Richard, Hall's Chronicle, and a long contemporary poem by Samuel Daniel entitled *The Civil War between York and Lancaster* all begin at the same point, the quarrel between Mowbray and Bolingbroke which led to the banishment of the latter and so gave the house of Lancaster a just pretext for their unjust seizure of power.

Strangely enough, however, before giving dramatic form to the events which led up to the Wars of the Roses, Shakespeare dealt with the Wars themselves and the monstrous tyranny which succeeded them. For as everyone knows, though he covered the whole period in a double cycle of eight plays — four on the rise and triumph of the usurping House of Lancaster, and four on its destruction at the hands of the House of York, which supplies more brutal usurpers than Bolingbroke himself — his earliest historical plays was the second cycle, which comprised the Three Parts of *Henry VI* and *Richard III*. Why he went to work in this somewhat preposterous fashion is anybody's guess. Mine is the guess propounded by Theobald and Malone in the 18th century and generally accepted until recently, *viz.*, that, being an actor-dramatist working from inside the theatre, Shakespeare began writing history plays because his company set him on to brighten up and tighten up plays by Greene or Peele on the troublous reign of Henry VI, which had come into their hands as bankrupt stock. Certain it is, at any rate, that he learnt to write history by endeavouring to impose the form and harmony of art upon the most confused

[4] cf. *Richard II*, 4, 1, 131, 242 ; 5, 1, 58.

Opposite. " This chair shall be my state, this dagger my sceptre, and this cushion my crown."
The other source of anxiety to Henry Bolingbroke. The hero prince is more often at Eastcheap than the court.

and difficult period in our history, the period lying between the accession of the infant Henry VI in 1421 and the defeat and death of Richard III in 1485. And one has only to compare the plays as he left them with diffuse and tangled accounts of the reigns of Henry VI and Richard III in the chronicles of Holinshed and Hall, who furnished the material out of which they were shaped, to realise how considerable his accomplishment was. Only one of the four, *Richard III*, it is true, still holds the stage, but to Londoners in the early nineties of the 16th century the *Henry VI* plays must have seemed astonishing productions, so far did they out-distance in strength and grip, in fluency and grace, anything of the kind seen before; eclipsing perhaps even Marlowe's *Tamburlaine the Great*, a twin drama of a very different kind, which had recently taken the town by storm, the storm of its thunderous rhetoric. Yet, however fresh the verse and original the dramaturgy, the political philosophy which is the burden of these plays was thoroughly conventional and is all to be found in Hall. But since it gives us the groundwork of Shakespeare's attitude towards history a few words must be said upon it, while a brief consideration of the plays themselves will help to a fuller understanding of the greater series which Shakespeare wrote later.

Under Henry V England attained a unity of purpose and height of power greater than at any other period of history known to the Elizabethans. In *Henry VI* Part I we see the French empire won at Agincourt utterly thrown away owing to the jealousies and factious treachery of the nobles that bore rule during the infancy and youth of Henry V's heir. Part II sets forth the domestic results of this same " intestine division " as Hall calls it, *viz.*, the temptation it offered on the one hand to an ambitious self-seeker like Richard Duke of York, and, on the other, to the forces of sheer anarchy such as the rabble Jack Cade leads to burn the Law Courts and sack Cheapside.

And in Part III faction has finally torn the commonwealth asunder.

In point of fact, Part I was an afterthought, written later than the other two Parts, which originally formed a single two-part play like 1 and 2 *Henry IV*, and entitled *The Contention between the Houses of York and Lancaster*. The Civil Wars themselves do not actually break out before the middle of this *Contention* play, *i.e.*, the end of what we now call 2 *Henry VI* or the beginning of its sequel. But a delightful " induction " to them is to be found in act 2 scene 4 of Part I, obviously supplied by Shakespeare to help link up the later written I *Henry VI* with the events of Part II and III. I refer to the Temple Garden scene. That the Wars of the Roses took their origin from a quarrel of law students in Temple Hall, and the plucking of white and red roses as badges of their opposing factions in the garden outside, has become a part of our tradition, and it may surprise some readers to learn that it has no warrant in the chronicles and probably sprang direct from the brain of Shakespeare; that is it in short a poetic myth invented to explain the badges which had quite another origin. That the scene was at any rate of Shakespeare's composition there can be no doubt, and it would be difficult to find anything more characteristic of his genius at this early period. Note for instance, how quickly it gets off the mark. Six players enter the bare Elizabethan stage and within six lines the whole situation and background have been brought before us. And what follows is of like quality. The scene is, in short, full of life and without a wooden line, a tawdy image, or a false note of any kind, though freely running into the quibbles and conceits which were Shakespeare's delight as this stage of his development. It is the scene of a writer brimming over with energy and self-confidence, above all of a born poet. I find it impossible to believe that much of the verse elsewhere in the Three Parts can have come from the same pen, especially in view of the trashy character of its imagery.

The episode which according to history, both Tudor and modern, marked the real outbreak of the Civil Wars was the Parliament of October, 1460, when Richard Duke of York openly asserted his claim to the crown, ascended the throne in Westminster Hall, and secured Henry VI's consent to his nomination as next in succession before the Prince of Wales. Such is the scene with which Part III commences. But the dramatist takes a high hand with history at the junction of Parts II and III, leaping from 1450 to 1455 in passing from act 4 to act 5 of Part II, and from the first battle of St. Albans in May, 1455 to the battle of Northampton in July, 1460 (or rather identifying these two battles), as he passes from one Part to the next.

During its first four acts Part II is concerned with two themes : (i) the removal and death of the young Henry's Protector, "the good Duke Humphrey" of Gloucester, at the instigation, or by the hands, of Margaret of Anjou, her lover the Earl of Suffolk, and the wicked Cardinal Beaufort ; and (ii) Cade's insurrection. The Cade scenes, which occupy most of Act 4, are excellent fooling : Shakespeare never created a more lively or entertaining crowd, while Cade himself for rascally self-complacency and gross ignorance makes a worthy fellow for Bottom and Dogberry. The insurrection fails, of course ; Cade is slain in the garden of Alexander Iden, an esquire of Kent ; and at first sight the whole episode seems to have little relevance to the main plot. The play is, however, held together, somewhat tenuously it is true, by the figure of York who, with his Machiavellian designs upon the crown, is shown secretly at work behind both Cade's rebellion and the downfall of Gloucester which precedes it.

Most of all this is from the modern point of view entirely

14

Opposite. " . . . For all the world,
As thou art at this hour was Richard then."
Prince Hal is recalled to his duty by his father, Bolingbroke.

unhistorical. So far from being a deep schemer Richard of York is now considered a man remarkably self-restrained and upright for his age, who only pressed his claim to the throne when it became clear that nothing less could save the country. On the other hand, Duke Humphrey, the wise counsellor and great patriot of 2 *Henry VI*, seems actually to have been the most arrogant and self-seeking of Henry's uncles, while there is no ground at all for charging Cardinal Beaufort with any responsibility for his death. Yet to the ultra-Protestant Hall the blackening of a cardinal's character was a praiseworthy deed, while the whitewashing of Humphrey made a worse case for the Yorkists and so suited the Tudor theory of history. The drama therefore had warrant on the whole in the chronicles for its appraisment of character, and, though it departed from them freely in many details, mainly by way of tightening up the plot and pulling its threads together, it very fairly represents the leading personalities, outstanding events, and general spirit of the period, as the Elizabethans understood them.

The last of the trilogy has little to offer the modern reader or spectator,[5] being for the most part a series of battles, and of the slanging-matches which invariably preceded battles on the Elizabethan stage, if not in the field itself. Yet, full as it is of coloured banners and the sound of trumpets, of high words and blazing passion, of hand to hand conflicts and ruthless stabbing, it gives once again a pretty fair picture of the state of the country, at any rate as the chroniclers saw it, between the Duke of York's bid for power in 1460 and the battle of Tewkesbury, followed by Henry VI's death in 1471. So "lated in the world" was England that she seemed altogether to have lost her way. And it is just this sense of forlorn helplessness that the plot — for there is a plot and one of some skill — seems

[5] Having since seen the interesting production of Part III at the Birmingham Repertory I should now phrase this differently. It is never safe for a scholar to generalise about a play until he has witnessed a production of it !

15

Opposite. " My due from thee is this imperial crown."
On Bolingbroke's deathbed, the prince
comes face to face with his destiny.

designed to bring out. King Henry sums it up in his famous soliloquy as he sits on the hill above Towton Field, watching his country's agony.

> Now sways it this way like a mighty sea
> Forced by the tide to combat with the wind ;
> Now sways it that way like the self-same sea
> Forced to retire by fury of the wind ;
> Sometime the flood prevails and then the wind ;
> Now one the better, then the other best ;
> Both tugging to be victors, breast to breast,
> Yet neither conqueror nor conquered :
> So is the equal poise of this fell war.

Of such equal poise indeed are the factions striving for the crown that a final decision seems beyond attainment and the agony for the nation as a whole is symbolised in this same scene by the entry first of " a son that has killed his father " and then of " a father that has killed his son," incidents directly suggested by a passage in Hall. Hall's too in part is the figure of the royal saint, as he seemed to Tudor England and still seemed to Wordsworth. For in accordance with their anti-Yorkist prejudices the Tudor historians wrote up Henry VI, as they had his uncle, Duke Humphrey, and even managed to throw a cloak over his insanity for a couple of centuries. To Shakespeare, on the other hand, are probably due the compassion, tenderness and love of his fellow man, which the sad King utters in speech after speech, as he moves through this world of passion and rancour, of shrieks and curses, of trunkless heads and the corpses of murdered children. Finally. in contrast to "holy Harry" we have the hunch-back, Richard of Gloucester, a human chaos born of social chaos, who symbolises, and in the next play rules, a monstrous England ; the inevitable term of the fell war, itself the inevitable outcome — as we are never allowed to forget — of the sacrilegious usurpation of Henry Bolingbroke.

16

Of that brilliant crook-play which we call *Richard III*,
I have space here to say two things only. First of all, directly
based as it is upon Sir Thomas Moore's unfinished *History of
King Richard III*,[6] itself the most brilliant piece of historical
writing yet seen in English, it is thus the joint-product of two
of the greatest of English spirits. We can indeed hardly
exaggerate what Shakespeare owes to Moore at this moment
of his development, and it is probably safe to say that it
equalled his debt to Plutarch later. And my second point
illustrates my first. In passing from *Henry VI* to *Richard III*
we seem to step straight from the middle ages into the modern
world, the world of the intrigues, counterplots, and sudden
executions that we now associate with the totalitarian state.
This is because the Nazis and Stalinites have brought back to
Europe the technique of Italian renaissance politics, and
Richard III is the earliest and most faithful reflection in English
drama of the fifteenth and early sixteenth century Italian
tyrants, about which Moore had heard much and whose most
sinister characteristics he freely transferred to Richard of
Gloucester, perhaps persuaded thereto by his friend and patron
Cardinal Morton, the bishop who fetches strawberries for
Richard in the play, and one of the chief agents of Richard's
overthrow in a actual history. Yet, as R. W. Chambers
points out, "with all its grim characterization of the last of
Yorkist King" Moore's *Richard III* " is not a piece of Lancastrian propaganda. Rather, it is an attack on the non-moral
statecraft of the early sixteenth century, exactly as *Utopia* is."
Seeing then that "Shakespeare's Richard is Moore's Richard"[7]
and that never was " non-moral statecraft " more rampant
than in our own times, Shakespeare's *Richard III* inevitably
possesses actuality for us which his other histories lack.

[6] Read by Shakespeare in the pages of Holinshed who transcribes it verbatim.

[7] R. W. Chambers, *Thomas More* p.117.

17

Let us now turn to Shakespeare's other great cycle, later in composition though earlier in historical time, the four plays seen at Stratford last summer. All that has been said above bears directly upon *Richard II*, the two *Henry IV* plays, and even to some extent upon *Henry V*, since the same Tudor philosophy of history inspires them all ; their creator shows himself conscious throughout of the terrible civil war that will follow upon Bolingbroke's sin ; and the audience for which they were written, or at least the politically mature among them, had in mind that such chaos might at any moment come again, inasmuch as the throne of England was occupied by an ageing spinster, and who would succeed her no one could tell, though her chief councillors William and Robert Cecil might guess when they put their heads together in utter secrecy. The criminal deposition and murder of King Richard is harped upon time and again in the plays that follow, while the fearful prophecy which the Bishop of Carlisle utters at the beginning of the deposition scene is echoed by the prayer which Bolingbroke's son utters on the eve of Agincourt and is, as we have seen, fulfilled to the letter in the reign of his grandson. All that is fundamental, the very stuff of Shakespeare's thought, as it was bound to be in an age when absolute monarchy, legitimacy, and "the divinity that doth hedge a king " seemed the only pillars of the social system.

This interpretation, together with the fact that Hall had already in 1548 " furnished the frame and stretched the canvas " for the whole eight plays, was first set forth in an Introduction to my edition of *Richard II* (1939). Since then a good deal, perhaps too much, had been heard about the matter, in particular from Dr. Tillyard and Dr. Lily Campbell, whose books on the history plays, one published in London (1944) and the other in California (1947), became something like " best sellers " in their respective countries. No doubt the ideas

18

Opposite. " You are right justice and you weigh this well."
The young king shows himself
magnanimous to the Lord Chief Justice.

and sentiments outlined above provided the main intellectual interest for "judicious" Elizabethan spectators of *Henry VI* and *Richard III*. But the spirit of Shakespeare was ever on the move, and he very rarely repeated himself, except in the use of certain technical devices and motives. I very much doubt therefore whether these ideas preoccupied either him or his audiences to the same extent in the plays on the rise of the House of Lancaster which belong to the years 1595-99. Certainly, upon that basic pattern of commonplace notions, his rapidly developing genius imposed new and more fascinating patterns and interests. There was first of all, and probably to his contemporaries first in importance, the astonishing depth and variety of character he now had at command. Richard II, Bolingbroke, and old York ; Hal, Hotspur, and Glendower ; Falstaff, Mistress Quickly, Doll Tearsheet, and Justice Shallow — to name principals only — all were more alive, more individual *voices*, than any in the earlier history plays, except perhaps Richard III. As for his predecessors and contemporaries, Marlowe and the rest, the figures in their plays shewed like squeaking puppets or a ventriloquist's dolls beside this troop of warm-blooded men and women, of all sorts and conditions. It is impossible to recapture, but impossible surely to overestimate, the excitement of London at these successive theatrical triumphs during the last five years of the 16th century ; though perhaps those who can remember how Shaw's plays burst upon the world in Granville-Barker's productions at the Court during the first five years of the 20th century may form some idea of it.

Then there was the interest provoked by a variety of dramatic types, of which the second series furnished no fewer than three. *Richard II* is Shakespeare's great political passion play, in which the Passion of the Gospel story is glanced at

Opposite. " My King, my Jove! I speak to thee my heart."
The newly crowned king puts his past behind him.

more than once, if distantly and in all reverence. *The Tragedie of King Richard the Second* is the tragedy of kingship. That the Monarch (" the Prince " was the Elizabethan term) wore a crown of cares, that his poorest and meanest subject might enjoy more peaceful sleep than he, was a constant theme with Shakespeare. You hear it from the lips of Henry VI, Henry IV, and Henry V in turn ; and Queen Elizabeth herself enlarged upon it in Parliament when it suited her purpose to sound a pathetic note. But the tragedy of *Richard II* was more than this : it depicts in moving pageant and in figured, coloured, and flowing verse, the agony and death of a sacrificial victim in the person of the Lord's anointed — of a semi-divine being as all kings appeared in those days, slain as it were upon the altar. Of course there is a good deal more in the play as well, but this is central, this one cannot doubt is what fascinated Shakespeare's contemporaries above all else. It was still doing so in the middle of the XIXth century ; for to Walter Pater, writing about productions by Charles Kean in the late fifties, the play seemed a great dramatic ritual and the " deposition " scene like

> " some long, agonising, ceremony, reflectively drawn out, with an extraordinary refinement of intelligence and variety of piteous appeal, but also with felicity of poetic invention, which puts these pages into a very select class, with the finest " vermeil and ivory " work of Chatterton or Keats."[8]

Does it do so today ? Much as I delighted in the skill and beauty of Mr. Redgrave's impersonation at Stratford I found I lacked, and I think a twentieth century audience must lack, the " king-worship " necessary for full sympathy with Richard in his fall and degradation.

If *Richard II* was Shakespeare's Tudor miracle play, the two parts of *Henry IV* was his great Tudor " morality," the con-

[8] *Appreciations*, p.198.

summation of a long series of sixteenth century " interludes of youth " or prodigal son dramas, in which the leading figure is a young scapegrace who, after sowing his wild oats in a number of highly entertaining scenes, repents in the most edifying manner imaginable. Shakespeare's youthful prodigal is the prodigal Prince, as Harry Monmouth already figured in the chronicles, who after repenting becomes the ideal king of English history. And the twin-play has other typical " morality " figures also : an old father from whom the royal " lusty juventus " is to inherit his property ; personified abstractions like Justice (the Lord Chief Justice), Chivalry (Hotspur), Lechery (Doll) ; and above all the Tempter — call him Vice, Devil, Lord of Misrule or what you will. Once this is realised, two things follow. First of all it is clear that the misleader of such a Prince must be a Tempter of an exceedingly fascinating kind. Shakespeare therefore summoned all his powers of invention and wit to the task of creating Falstaff — and succeeded so well that his modern critics blame the Prince, not for consorting with the old ruffian, but for having the heart, or rather the heartlessness to break free of him. And it follows, in the second place, that the audiences for whom Shakespeare wrote the play, being accustomed to the " morality " tradition, no more thought of questioning or deploring the downfall and arrest of Falstaff at the end than their fathers would have questioned or deplored the spectacle of the Vice being carried off to Hell at the conclusion of a religious play.

Nor do I think those who applauded Mr. Quayle's Falstaff last summer were unduly cast down by the finale of 2 *Henry IV*, so completely had he mastered the character in all aspects the two Parts reveal and so justly and skilfully had he interpreted them. My only regret was that he allowed the fat knight himself to appear cast down once and at this last moment only.

21

Was that "confident brow" ever browbeaten ? or could that "throng of words, that came with such more than impudent sauciness" from him, be checked and put to silence by "Father Antic the law ?" The Devil they could ! He should have been *carried* off by force, struggling with the officers and indignantly protesting "My lord, my lord" until out of earshot. What is it Milton puts into the mouth of his ancestor, and tragic counterpart, the Prince of Darkness ?

> All is not lost ; th'unconquerable will,
> And courage never to submit or yield.

Read "wit" for "will" and you have the irrepressible spirit of the Prince of Comedy.

As for the notion already glanced at, a notion entertained by many famous critics, that Henry V was a prig and a cad, I make bold to assert that anything so absurd could never have crossed the minds of either Shakespeare or his audience. To them Henry of Monmouth was the ideal representative of order and security as Richard Crookback had been of chaos and national disaster. They knew by experience that England's only safeguard against internal strife and "the envy of less happier lands" was a Prince who, with the sceptre firmly in his grasp, could be the adored leader of a united and harmonious commonweal, in which noble, merchant, yeoman and peasant worked together for the good of the whole. Such a Prince was their own Queen Elizabeth ; such a Prince was Shakespeare's Henry of Monmouth. And he had accomplished something more than was possible to her ; she defended England against the might of Spain, but he conquered France ! For such a hero, whom "no emperor in magnanimity ever excelled," as Hall tells us, a special kind of drama was needed and Shakespeare invented one for him in the epical play he called *The Life of Henry V*, a play in which the character only second in prominence to that of the hero

22

is the so-called Chorus who " presents " the hero to us at the various stages of his glorious career, a character I believe which Shakespeare himself played before Queen Elizabeth.

One point more to round off this summary account of Shakespeare's constitutional theory as shown in the English Histories, a point not I think generally apprehended. For all his greatness, sternness, and ruthless determination, Henry V was no despot; there was a power in England above him, the Rule of Law. And Shakespeare is careful to make this perfectly plain. For when he shows him to us first as king after the death of Henry IV, what does he make him say ?

> This is the English not the Turkish court ;
> Not Amurath an Amurath succeeds,
> But Harry Harry !

After which he turns to the Lord Chief Justice, commends him for sending him to prison in his madcap days, and thus concludes :

> There is my hand.
> You shall be as a father to my youth,
> My voice shall sound as you do prompt mine ear,
> And I will stoop and humble my intents.
> To your well-practised wise directions.

In a word, above the throne itself sat justice. Here too Shakespeare was giving utterance to one of the political assumptions of the Elizabethan age. But hardly of the Jacobean. For so far from " humbling his intents " to any directions of his Lord Chief Justice, James Stuart dismissed him from office and so laid the axe at the root of his dynasty, and even for a while of the monarchy itself.[9] Perhaps this was one reason why Shakespeare left English history alone — except for that pageant play *Henry VIII* — after the death of the great Queen.

[9] cf. A. L. Rowse, *The England of Elizabeth* (1950), p.382.

THE PLAYS AT STRATFORD

by

T. C. WORSLEY

★

THE CONCEPTION

As STRATFORD's special contribution to the Festival of Britain, the Director decided to stage a cycle of those four historical plays which chronologically follow one upon the other — *Richard II*, *Henry IV*, Parts I and II, and *Henry V*. It is generally agreed, he suggested in a foreword, that " These plays form a tetralogy and were planned as one great play. They present not only a living epic of England through the reign of the three kings, but are also a profound commentary on Kingship."

Henry V, the Director argued, was the true hero of the whole play, " Henry V who personified to the people of Shakespeare's England, the ideal king: brave, warlike, generous, just." But Henry does not appear until the second play. *Richard II*, then, constitutes a kind of prologue. Henry Bolingbroke, father of Henry V, was the first successful usurper since William the Conqueror, though he himself did not live to see his line safely established. In order to establish this line he had to smash the mediaeval conception of King-ship which had lasted since the Conquest. " Richard II as king, represented the power of God on earth: he was His minister, ' the deputy elected by the Lord '." His deposition and murder " represent a break with an old order: but they also embody a curse." Both Henry Bolingbroke and his son are to be haunted all their reigns by Richard's death (just as,

24

it is suggested, Elizabeth's reign was shadowed by the execution of Mary, Queen of Scots).

In treating the plays as a cycle, then, the emphasis in *Richard II* leans more strongly towards this political aspect than it would if the play were acted on its own. The personal tragedy of Richard which commonly dominates the play must give equal room to the drama of Bolingbroke's usurpation. For it is Bolingbroke, on the political plain, who is to dominate the next two parts. With *Henry IV* the true hero makes his first appearance. But Prince Hal does not grow into heroic stature until *Henry V*. " To his father he seems the most unstable of allies, and the king's heart yearns to have as his son the most notable of his enemies, Harry Hotspur." For the prophecies spoken at the end of *Richard II* have now come true. The usurper is now in the same position as Richard was — assailed by rebels; and he has to face them without the support of that sacred principle of Kingship to which Richard might, had he but had the courage, have appealed. He has to face them, too, without the support of his son who is climbing to his own stature in his own peculiar way — in the taverns of East London with Falstaff and his companions. True, father and son are reconciled by the end of the play. But how much that reconciliation is worth still remains unknown to the father.

Even by the end of Part II, the father must remain uncertain — for at the very last, on his deathbed, when he fancies Hal to have seized the crown before his actual death, his old doubts are revived.

At long last in *Henry V* the hero comes into his own. But we, who have fresh in our minds his long ascent, will not take him too uncritically as the schoolboy pattern hero. " Shakespeare is at no particular pains to idealise him entirely: he lets us see that Hal inherits some of his father's political

25

astuteness and even ruthlessness, he lets us see a king who can lose his temper with a common soldier. He lets us see a man. A man who, more than any other of the monarchs whom Shakespeare dramatised, possessed some at least of the qualities of a great king including that of the greatest quality: that of having and holding his people's love."

II

Such in outline was the conception which animated this presentation of the four plays as one cycle. In closer detail this conception requires a number of shifts in emphasis as against the ordinary practice of playing the plays each as a separate entity. Perhaps, as I have already hinted, the most marked change is in the treatment of *Richard II*. For this play lends itself especially to individual performance. Yet treating it as the prologue of the cycle does bring many unexpected rewards. I am myself in a particularly good position to say this, because I started out with a prejudice against the notion.

At the outset *Richard II* seemed to me difficult to fit in to the scheme, for it differs entirely from the other three in being an " inward " drama. The other three — so I remembered them — seemed to me to deal with practical extroverted characters, and to deal with them in the way particularly suited for such — the chronicle method. While *Richard II* seemed to me to be written in a different style — one that foreshadows the great tragedies. But having experienced the cycle as a cycle, I now confess to finding that much in *Richard II* that seems wasteful and otiose when we consider it singly, is extremely pointful when we connect it up with its successors.

Treated as a play complete in itself *Richard II* is the personal tragedy of the king — the overthrow from within of a weak

26

Opposite. " As I am a soldier, A name that in my thoughts becomes me best . . ." The king leads his army to the walls of Harfleur.

poetic nature; and that personal tragedy is the whole interest of the play. Yet in that case, one must notice, the play only gets into its real stride in the third act. The first two acts are too long an introduction to this interior tragedy, and there is a split in the character drawing. The treatment of Richard by the dramatist alters at that third act. In the first two acts one can only feel for him, at most, a removed pity — the pity one may feel at watching any self-destructive character in the process of destroying itself. But then from the third act on — from Richard's return from Ireland to find himself friendless in England — the nature of the treatment changes. Now one sees Richard, the person, from the inside, and one feels for him from the inside. In his language he distills the very essence of adolescent self-pity, and we are caught right into his personal tragedy, and we may, when the play is isolated, from then on experience the tragedy in the same kind of mode as we experience the later tragedies.

But when *Richard II* was played as the first part of the cycle, the case was different. The split in the character remains, but its effect is diminished, because our interest in the political events of the whole period which the four plays are to cover is going to be equally as sharp as our interest in the personal dramas. Indeed the political thread is doubly important in *Richard II*, for all the politics of the three following plays are the direct result of — and so echo and parallel — what happens here. The first two acts of *Richard II* may seem a long prologue to the personal tragedy of Richard. But they are not, and do not seem, a long prologue to the whole cycle. They show us the behaviour of the last of the kings who is claiming the Divine Right, and why and how that behaviour led to his overthrow. This is an essential introduction, and it is most dramatically stated.

The political scenes, then, in *Richard II* must be heavily

27

weighted, for it is they which are to provide the continuity. In terms of drama this means that Bolingbroke must, if he can, make an impression on us no less deep than Richard himself does. When the play is played separately, it is customary to diminish the audience's sympathy with Bolingbroke by making him arrogant and over-weening, giving him an un-sympathetic touch of hauteur, and by correspondingly heightening our sympathy for Richard. In the cycle this process must be reversed. The Richard must not engage too predominating a share of our sympathy (and those first two acts where he is exhibited as a petulant spiteful adolescent have their use here), while the Bolingbroke must, in contrast, win us by his dignity, nobility and virility.

For it is Bolingbroke who bridges the first gap, Bolingbroke who holds up to us the pattern of Kingship until his son is ready to take over from him; and it is on Bolingbroke that the political thread running through the first three plays hangs. And there is another point here. When we see *Henry IV*, Part I on its own, we come upon Bolingbroke already the accepted king threatened with a rebellion, and righteously de-nouncing the enemies of the throne; and we may easily forget in that splendid rhetoric the facts of his case. But coming straight to this play from *Richard II*, we cannot do that. We cannot escape being conscious that he is himself only a usurper, hoist now with his own petard. For, there, opposed to him now, is that very Northumberland who was his chief ally in unseating Richard. Henry Bolingbroke — whatever he may say — is on the throne by virtue of nothing but force of arms; and he stays there only by force, and in so far as his personal qualities earn him the place. We cannot take him for granted (as we do when we see the play on its own); actor and pro-ducer have to establish him: and establish him, so to speak, against the facts.

28

By this time the hero of the play, Prince Hal, has arrived on the scenes. In viewing him we have the great advantage of the long sweep. Actions and behaviour which, in the short run, might count too much against him have time and space to be viewed in proper proportions. His development is slow, but we can afford to wait for its gradual growth. But meanwhile there are dangers to be guarded against, and pre-conceptions to be broken down. Harry Hotspur first. He is commonly presented as the hero of *Henry IV*, Part I. His courage, dash and chivalry throw Hal's actions into the worst light (and in that case Hal's " conversion " often seems to be too sudden to be convincing and our sympathy remains, as Hazlitt's did, with Hotspur). We cannot afford that to happen here. Hotspur must shine, but he must not outshine Hal.

Then, again, Falstaff is a danger. This character has al-ready so endeared itself to us, has so established the myth of loveableness, that we easily fall into sentimentalising him. Once that is done, our sympathy for Hal is weakened; we lean towards Falstaff, and begin to think our hero something of a prig. An unsentimental Falstaff is, perhaps, easier to accept in our day than in any other, for we have a special weakness for rogues of all kinds, where other ages have always had to apologise for their pleasure in the old ruffian. An old ruffian, to put it at its crudest, must be the basis of the interpretation of Falstaff here, and, whatever else is added, that basis must always remain clearly visible.

By Part II these dangers will have passed. Hotspur is dead, and the Prince is already sufficiently divided from Falstaff for us to link him more definitively with his destiny. That destiny, since it is what we are leading up to — and since preparation is the essence of drama — must be evident in its kernel from the very beginning. From the first Hal must

29

show himself conscious of it and we must get the impression from the Hal that, whatever comes in between, he is capable of his moment when the moment arrives. This feeling will grow and grow upon us gradually as the plays progress. Bolingbroke, even on his deathbed, may still be in doubt. But we — and this will add immeasurably to the pathos of the scene — by that time must have no doubts at all. We have seen the follies of the Prince of Wales, but we have judged and evaluated the spirit in which he has indulged in them. We have measured him against Harry Hotspur and had reason to prefer the Prince. As we trace the slow development of his character we shall see the hero emerging, and so we will already know that, when the moment comes, he will have to reject his boon companion, and we shall never doubt that he is at heart the kind of young man who must make the right choice, the choice that leads to Henry V.

So Hal ascends the throne. But the Hal whom we have followed from Eastcheap and Gadshill is not, and cannot be quite the customary Henry V, the rousing patriotic hero. He has grown into the hero, true. But still close about him cling the phases through which he has passed. The position changes the man: and he rises to the position. But we are more conscious than usual of the man behind the king, because we have fresher in our minds than usual the boy behind the man. The incident with the soldier, to take the Director's example, is not for us simply one of those acts of royal condescension which propaganda will re-tell to show that this king, too, does not disdain the " common touch." It is an act which takes us back in memory to Falstaff and Poins and Francis the drawer, to that turbulent adolescence out of which our hero has now emerged.

30

Opposite. " . . . Six frozen winters spent
Return with welcome home from banishment."
Richard sentences the young Bolingbroke.

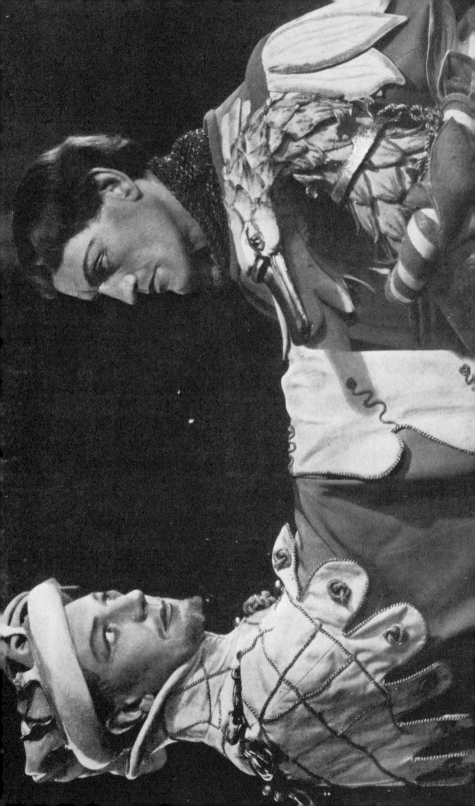

THE CONCEPTION IN ACTION

ONLY AN organisation such as Stratford has now become would be capable of presenting these four plays in this way. Continuity is the essence of the presentation, and three conditions are necessary to achieve it. First, a controlling director who can fit the four productions into his conception. Then, a permanent set which remains unchanged throughout, to give us the illusion of unity of place. Thirdly, a set of actors who can carry from play to play those roles which overlap: and this not just in the major roles, Bolingbroke, Hal, Falstaff, but no less in the subsidiary parts, Northumberland, Westmorland, Lady Percy, and the characters from low life.

Miss Tanya Moiseiwitsch was chosen to design the costumes and the set. The set consisted of a large central wooden structure, placed mid-stage, with a platform at the top and a set of stairs leading down round each side of it to the main stage. In the centre of this structure were two doors which provided a central entrance, or which served, as the needs dictated, as an inner recess. The set had to serve many different purposes, and it was embellished as occasion demanded with props or with hangings, to suggest at different times, inn scenes, palaces, gardens and so on, the structure itself being of plain unvarnished oak. Structurally, the set was extremely practical; it provided three acting spaces and a large variety of entrances; it allowed the action to move in an uninterrupted flow.

There was one other permanent feature — the throne, set down at the side by the proscenium arch. And just as the political business of the plays centred round it, so, in the absence of a curtain, it was the first thing which was gradually illuminated to mark the beginning of each play.

The large company was a particularly strong one in the important middle reaches; so that the subsidiary roles were

31

in experienced hands. But, as well, the minor parts right down to the members of the crowd and walkers-on were filled by young actors who had been, many of them, trained at Stratford for several seasons; and the stage management had in the previous years gained experience in the large scale productions to which Stratford has committed itself lately. All this meant an unusual efficiency and high state of discipline which is essential in this kind of production.

There remained the casting of the major roles, which turned out to be particularly happy. For Bolingbroke, Mr. Quayle had available Mr. Harry Andrews, an experienced Shakespearean actor who had been growing in stature and weight through three seasons at Stratford and who was now at the height of his form and ready for the great role which Bolingbroke constitutes in the long first three-quarters of the cycle. Noble, dignified, manly, impressive, Mr. Andrews provided in his appearance alone exactly the right gravity and weight for this conception of Bolingbroke. And his fine measured acting was to bring to the role as nearly a perfect realisation of Mr. Quayle's intentions as he could possibly have hoped for.

Mr. Quayle himself took Falstaff and since the whole conception was his own, there was no danger there that the equilibrium would be upset by a leaning towards the sentimental. For Prince Hal, Mr. Richard Burton was chosen. This was, doubtless, at the outset a choice involving a certain risk. Mr. Burton is a young actor who had shown already that he had that curious indefinable magnetism which is termed " star quality." This would ensure that, whatever else, he would draw the audience effectively with him whatever he did. It was clever to see, too, that he was just the actor to give us from the start a slightly different picture of Hal from the usual, that he would infuse, by that far-away Welsh look of his, a different element from the customary cheerful wild-oat sowing. But it must have been, in the producer's mind, a matter of uncertainty whether he would be able to rise to the man of action and to the rhetoric in *Henry V*, whether the voice would ring out full and clear in the great patriotic speeches. If perhaps in the end it didn't, Mr. Burton did succeed in imposing a highly consistent reading of the part which carried in its own way right through.

Finally, Mr. Quayle was blessed in his choice of the star actor for the season. The parts taken by Mr. Michael Redgrave were, for the cycle as a whole, subsidiary. Richard and Hotspur are the major roles when the plays are given individually. But the whole point of playing them in cycle was that they must not be allowed to be here. If they had completely dominated, then the whole enterprise would have got off on the wrong foot. Only a star actor of great unselfishness would be prepared to mute his performance of traditionally star roles in the interest of a wider conception. Mr. Redgrave is just the very actor who would see the importance of the point and be prepared to fit in.

And so the set is built, the brilliant costumes designed and executed, the company assembled and rehearsed. The next question is how this conception of the plays as a single unit, a cycle, would strike the audiences. Well, first it must be remembered that the playing in cycle only affects certain aspects of the plays, and that the differences are more strongly marked at the beginning than at the end. The presentation of *Richard II* is considerably modified, that of *Henry V* hardly at all. Next it must be remembered that the point would only be clear to anyone who saw the plays in four successive performances, and withheld judgement on the beginning until he had seen the end. Many visitors and many critics were only able to sample one play, or one play at a time. These inevitably lost the full effect, and may even have been puzzled

33

by emphases and production points which were intelligible enough in terms of the four plays as a single unit. So, I propose, before recording the reception of the individual plays, to give an account of how this treatment of the plays affected my response to them as I reconsidered them after seeing the plays in four successive performances. I shall leave aside for the moment the very interesting question propounded by the Director whether the plays really were planned by Shakespeare as one great play. Planned or not, the playing of them as if they were did make for striking differences of emphasis, in the relations of the main characters, and it may be of some interest to record what the effect of these seemed to me to be.

RICHARD II

WHEN WE conceive of *Richard II* as the prologue to the cycle we have to adjust our feelings about it radically. It becomes less the tragedy of Richard himself and more the Rise of Bolingbroke. Politically it represents the struggle between a new and an old conception of Kingship, and this struggle is dramatised in a personal struggle between Bolingbroke and Richard. The drama is only strengthened by the fact that the upholder of the old conception is weak and the upholder of the new strong.

The importance of the first two acts is very great in setting the scene, placing the factions and rivalries and displaying the currents of opinions that are dividing hearts and loyalties. Some of these differences are pointed at the very opening in distinctions of dress and of bearing. The play opens in the king's palace where a council of state has been summoned. The first to enter are the nobles who talk among themselves, until the king and his entourage come in. The king takes up the orb and sceptre, and mounts the spot-lighted throne with

34

Opposite. " These words hereafter thy tormentors be!"
The dying Gaunt upbraids the king.

his followers grouped around him. The elegance of the royal party now calls attention to the fact that the nobles, by contrast, are plain men, plainly dressed in russets and dull reds and greens: dressed plainly, but not meanly. It is, in fact, the kind of plainness of which plain men are proud. While the epicene king and his followers are dandies, dressed in pastel pinks, light blues and golds. They parade their jewelry; they are frenchified. The plain men's plainness may easily be imagined to be a kind of unspoken protest against this frippery.

The king speaks in an affected mince. Gaunt, whom he first calls out, answers him in an unaffected regional accent. Accidents of casting will not allow the regional accent to be accurate: and Gaunt's Welsh may at first strike strangely on the ear. But it soon ceases to, and the point — a very good one — remains (it is to be underlined later): the speech of the nobles in their different local pronunciations reminds us that at this time they lived away in their own provinces retaining the manners and customs and individuality of their own localities. They come to London, most of them, only when they are summoned on affairs of State, as they are now in this matter of the quarrel between Mowbray and young Bolingbroke. These two, as they now take the centre of the stage, particularise a little further these generalisations. Thomas Mowbray is a soldier, not a courtier, simple, sincere, direct and plain. But Bolingbroke — and we may have noticed the same of Gaunt — being of the blood royal, is less plain than the plain men, though not gaudy like the king's followers. He is of the court, but not of *this* court. Spiritually he belongs with the plain men — is a young man of the old virtues. He has their nobility without their plainness; and out of it he despises the king.

For already in the first scenes the nature of the personal

35

Opposite. " Of comforts no man speak."
Richard returns to England to find himself friendless.

antagonism between these two is foreshadowed. It is lightly stressed in Bolingbroke's first words to the king:

> " Many years of happy days befall
> My gracious sovereign, my most loving liege."

There is an easily discernible irony in the emphasis Mr. Harry Andrews puts on that " most loving." And this irony Richard returns later in giving Mowbray leave to speak:

> " Were he my brother, nay, my kingdom's heir,
> As he is but my father's brother's son,"

the last line pointed directly at Bolingbroke. Our sympathy in these early scenes can hardly but be with the noble virile figure Mr. Harry Andrews presents as the young Bolingbroke. There is, it is true, a touch of arrogance, but it is youthful arrogance, justifiable in view of the treatment he receives from the king. This treatment is worse than unjust, it is frivolous. For while Mowbray and Bolingbroke are opposed in a quarrel that concerns not only their honour but their very lives, Richard would, if he could, smile the whole thing away:

> " Forget, forgive, conclude and be agreed:
> Our doctors say this is no month to bleed."

And the entourage sycophantically laugh at these inadequate little pleasantries.

Yet behind the personal struggle there is, equally important, a political struggle on foot. The principle of Kingship as a sacred inalienable function is what Richard stands upon. " Lions make leopards tame." It is the divine right that makes Richard a lion and he remains a lion by virtue of that even if he proves in his own person a feeble one. It is the principle itself that is now to be attacked and, by the end of the play, overthrown. Here at the beginning this principle is not even challenged from the outside, though it is threatened from within. A lion, to remain a lion, must act the lion. It is no good merely to roar:

" We were not born to sue but to command."—

if the moment after you admit:

" Which since we cannot do . . . "

The principle, in fact, is to be betrayed through the weakness of its chief officer, and it is this which is to make the drama. Yet, still at this time there is enough common goodwill behind that principle for it to have been maintained if Richard had been strong. In the little scene which follows this, the old Duchess of Gloucester is rebuked — when she cries out for individual vengeance against Richard — by Gaunt who has as much reason as she to fight the king on personal grounds, but who stands for the old values:

" God's is the quarrel: for God's substitute,
His deputy anointed in His sight,
Hath caused his death: the which if wrongfully
Let heaven revenge: for I may never lift
An angry arm against His minister."

The king is God's substitute, His minister; his orders and acts have the authority of the divine.   To oppose him is to oppose God.

The sacred principle is not directly challenged until Boling-broke's return from exile. In the scene at the lists — when the fight is stopped by the king throwing down his warder and the king descends and pronounces sentence — his authority is still not questioned. Bolingbroke accepts his sentence with the same contemptuous irony he has displayed earlier. For at least the lion has acted, has asserted his lionship, and no one as yet directly questions his authority. Even Mowbray feels that the struggle is on a purely personal level — as in one aspect it is — and his prophecy when he throws back Bolingbroke's last accusation in his face, lingers in the mind

37

long later:

"But what thou art, God, thou and I do know;
And all too soon, I fear, the king shall rue."

The issue is forced by the king's recklessly flippant behaviour over John of Gaunt's death. Gaunt on his deathbed felt justified in attacking the king with a violence that he never dared use before. But it is the king's behaviour that he attacks: not his kingship. That the old order cannot question. Gaunt's brother, York, now at Gaunt's death the last surviving of the Black Prince's sons, is left to carry this principle on shoulders all to weak to support it. Richard's immediate seizure of Gaunt's property at the moment of the announcement of his death is almost more than he can bear. He takes the trimmer's course, "I'll not be by the while": but he can't escape his responsibility by turning his head away, and with a fine stroke of ironic humour Richard fixes it more firmly on him by creating him Lord Governor during his absence in Ireland.

All this time standing by, solid, large, immovable, expressionless, has been the most representative imaginable of the plain men from the distant provinces, Northumberland. He has said almost nothing. He has watched the tantrums of the childish king with all the plain man's scorn for the neurotic. He has not intervened. But he *has* decided. The middle generation of the older order has made up its mind in him. The principle of Divine Right is no longer sovereign. This king, this representative of it, has made it impossible. When the king and his followers go out, the plotting begins.

Such, in outline, was the impression which the production of these first two acts conveyed to us. A number of slight shifts of emphasis brought them forward as the introduction not just to this play but to the whole cycle. Notably, the principle at stake was always underlined so that it made a

38

clear impact unobscured by the personalities in the fore-ground. The pageantry of the court was particularly dig-nified and solemn to reinforce upon us that the king as person is only incidental to the king as function. The one direct personal clash, that between the king and Gaunt,— beautifully produced to a mounting climax — remained lucidly a *personal* clash. The majesty of the king as king, and the respect paid to his sovereignty, were carefully emphasised, however wilfully and childishly Richard himself behaved. This childishness of the king's — his tears of temper and his bored impatience with York's reminiscences of the Black Prince — was played up unsparingly by Mr. Redgrave; and its alternation with moments of regal dignity and command suggested exactly the right con-bination of instability and regality to contrast with the even dignity of Mr. Andrews' youthful Bolingbroke. A few touches of production for him — like the solemn lengthening of his exit line:

" Where'er I wander, boast of this I can,
Though banished, yet a true born Englishman "—

establish him firmly in our sympathy and prepare us for his taking a central position from now on.

For in the grand sweep it is Bolingbroke who is the main character, not Richard; and we must be persuaded to watch him no less intently for the rest of this play than we watch Richard himself. How Bolingbroke rises to his situation is as important as how Richard falls to his. So it is Bolingbroke who opens the second part, a Bolingbroke who we notice at once has grown, physically and spiritually, in the years of exile. There is a greater weight about him now. The chin has put on a beard and the youthful arrogance has become dignity. Foremost among his followers is that same proud Northumberland. He is a little less plain now than he was before. He has learned to flatter his new master, though he doesn't do it very well. Or is there now a slight irony in *his* tone, foreshadowing the change in him? From the political point of view this scene where Bolingbroke finds Richard with only a handful of followers in Flint castle is the centre of the play. It is here that the cause is lost, the old principle of kingship destroyed by the vacillation of its last champion. And the production, rightly for its purpose, plays the scene with exaggerated weight and deliberation. For at the outset it seems as if the principle can be maintained if only Richard will believe in it himself. But the disasters that have befallen him one after the other seem to have unmanned him and by now this principle is only a kind of literary fancy with which to bemuse himself:

" Not all the water in the rough rude sea
     Can wash the balm from an anointed king . . .
     God for his Richard hath in heavenly pay
     A glorious angel . . ."

The phrases are fine but (Mr. Redgrave manages to convey in his style of delivering them) the power has leaked out of them. He uses then as conjurations:

" I had forget myself: am I not king?
     Awake thou coward majesty . . .

and they conjure up nothing but disaster. If they still really meant anything to him, they might still work. For this meeting between Bolingbroke and the king is the final test of their validity. The issue is still theoretically open. Boling-broke and his followers still claim that they come only for their due. The imperturbable Northumberland, it is true, regards the whole thing with a certain contempt, as play acting. When he goes forward to bear the king a greeting from Bolingbroke and is chidden by Richard for not kneeling to the sacred majesty, he doesn't drop to his knee, he just stands there insolently, immovably, and lets the gush of words flow past him. Not so, though, Bolingbroke. By another fine stroke of production he, when Richard descends, tells his followers to show all due respect to the king, and he himself performs a wonderfully elaborate triple obeisance in front of the man who still must be regarded as his leige lord. And the exchange that follows between them is made to carry an enormous weight as if it were two or three times longer than the single page of text which is all it really is.

Bol: My gracious Lord I come but for my own.

K. Rich: Your own is yours, and I am yours and all.

Bol: So far be mine, my most redoubted Lord
           As my true service shall deserve your love.

K. Rich: Well you deserve: they well deserve to have
           That know the strong'st and surest way to get . . .
           What you will have, I'll give and willing too
           For do we must what force will have us do.

The change in Bolingbroke is now pronounced. The arrogance has gone and the contempt with it. He is almost gentle with the king. The irony is now all on Richard's side — an irony, Mr. Redgrave makes us feel, that springs from self-pity. But the great impression of this scene is that we are made to feel that Richard might still up to the last words gain something out of the wreck, if he had any longer the will. It is that he lacks. He puts his own defeat into Bolingbroke's mouth:

K. Rich: Set on towards London, cousin, is it so?

Bol: Yea, my good Lord.

K. Rich: Then I must not say no.

That scene is the turning point. Bolingbroke has now seized power: and from now on through the rest of this play and into the two parts of *Henry IV* we shall watch him reaping the results of his breaking of the ancient principle, to which process, in the longer view, the deposition and murder of Richard is only incidental. Crime, accusation and counter-accusation, plot and counter-plot. The play began with this and Bolingbroke's reign is to begin with it. Bolingbroke ascends the throne as Henry IV, but even as he does so he knows that he steps into a louring world of enmity:

> " Little are we beholding to your love,
> And little looked for at your helping hands."

If the deposition scene belongs largely and rightly to Richard, all the same Bolingbroke is never allowed to sink back into unimportance. So decidedly and impressively has he been built up for us that we are conscious throughout Richard's eloquent dramatics of Bolingbroke *growing* there on the throne, as, without speaking, his eyes follow the deposed king's every action. The other central character, Northumberland, has also grown meanwhile; but where Bolingbroke grows in nobility and stature, Northumberland grows only in arrogance, as if power were almost visibly rising to his head. The mastery with which these two characters have been built up for us is indicated by the force with which the respective adjectives Richard applies to them strike us when they come. " Mark, *silent* king " he says to Bolingbroke. " No lord of thine, thou *haught insulting* man " he cries at Northumberland. And in each case — it is the result of careful preparation of course, as if these epithets had been taken from the first as key phrases and scene by scene been built up to — the description comes as a kind of confirmatory seal on what we have been feeling about them.

This is only another way of saying that for the special purposes of this production Northumberland and especially Bolingbroke — subsidiary roles ordinarily speaking — have to be kept, and are kept, in the centre of the picture. The

42

Opposite. " Thou see'est I have more flesh than another man and therefore more frailty." Falstaff accuses Hal of picking his pocket.

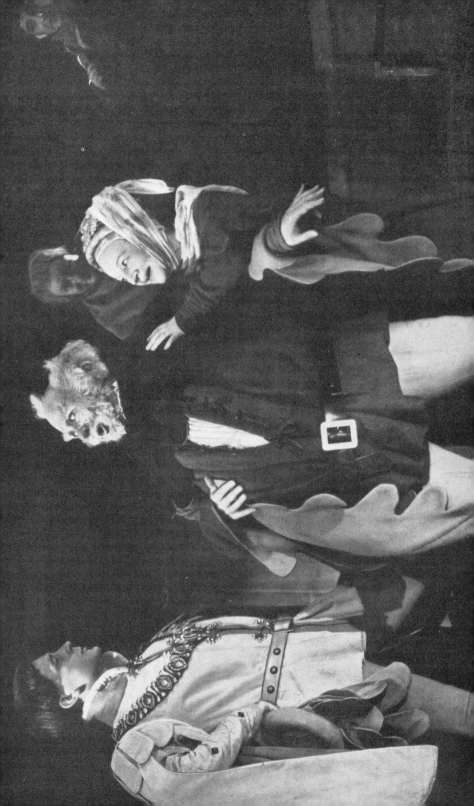

emphasis cannot be allowed to come down too heavily on Richard, for he here makes his last appearance while the others go on. This is the main difference between a production of the cycle and a production of the play by itself. And here the success with which the producer achieved this shift of emphasis is demonstrated by the fact that he did it in spite of a drastic cut which worked against his idea. The whole of the sub-plot describing Aumerle's treachery and his arrival at his father's house, York's discovery of the plot and the scene where he with his Duchess and Aumerle plead with Bolingbroke — this scene, which would have helped to reinforce the weight on Bolingbroke, was sacrificed. The result might easily have been to tip the balance dangerously at the end towards the interior drama of the play, with Richard's long prison scene coming so close after deposition. But in fact this did not happen. Careful production, together with the very great weight and dignity which Mr. Andrews put into Bolingbroke, established him sufficiently for his final rejection of Piers Exton, short though it is, to make a full effect and to leave Bolingbroke at the end of the play a lonely and noble figure in the forefront of our minds.

THE HENRYS

WE LEFT Bolingbroke at the end of *Richard II* a dominating figure; and politically it is he who dominates the two parts of *Henry IV*. The contention and civil strife which had already begun before Richard's deposition is the note on which the new play opens, and this theme is to alternate with the growth of Prince Hal throughout the two parts of *Henry IV*. In the playing and the producing of Bolingbroke himself there is no particular difference to mark when the plays are given in the cycle from when they are presented singly, though there is, of course, a very marked difference in the way the audience,

43

coming straight to this play fresh from *Richard II*, view him.

There is a longish time lag between *Richard II* and *Henry IV, Part I*. In the interval the young Bolingbroke has grown into middle age. But it is the same man, increased as we were led to expect in the first play, in authority and command. Now it is his turn to suffer the blows that he inflicted upon Richard, and foremost among his enemies is that same Northumberland whom we have just come from seeing as his chief ally in his rise. The irony of this situation pointed in many echoes and allusions to the first play strikes home to us very forcibly. Bolingbroke himself is most conscious of the irony of this situation in relation to his own son Hal. In all three of the big scenes in these two parts where father and son meet, Bolingbroke is haunted by the idea that Hal is now playing the same role that Richard played in relation to him years before:

> " The skipping king, he ambled up and down,
>   With shallow jesters, and rash bavin wits,
>   Soon kindled and soon burnt; carded his state,
>   Mingled his royalty with capering fools,
>   Had his great name profaned with their scorns. . .
>   And in that very line, Harry, standest thou,
>   From thou hast lost thy princely privilege
>   With vile participation."

This identification of Hal with Richard strikes the audience, who have seen both, as quite beside the mark. But that Bolingbroke in his old age should make it, emerges as an acute piece of observation by the dramatist, which unless the plays are seen in a cycle we would be likely to miss.

The two ways in which, in playing the plays as a cycle, distinct differences have to be made are in the treatment of Hotspur and the treatment of Falstaff. It is customary when playing *Henry IV* singly for Harry Hotspur to assume the hero's role. But in this production a conception of Hotspur

44

has to be found which will be congruent with all that we hear about him, but yet will be someting quite different from the usual admired romantic. It was just this which the producers and Mr. Michael Redgrave, the actor, found for us. First, this Hotspur speaks a kind of rough Doric, and is proud of it. He is very decidedly one of the men from the distant provinces taking pride in the roughness of spirit which this has bred in him. And this is the basis of his contempt for the Court. He is a fighter and a little too much of the boaster. We can't help admiring his spirit and attack, but that over-plus of bragging is just what prevents us preferring him to Hal. This Hotspur is a little too pleased with his own uncouthness. The modesty that Hal in his turn shows contrasts agreeably with it. Not that we dislike Hotspur. On the contrary, there is something winning about his tempestuousness, his going on and on and on, after the king has withdrawn, aiming his fiery anger at the empty throne until even his fellow conspirators are bored with him, although that does not stop him. He is a glowing ember and he must burn himself out. It is in this heat that he produces the first of those ironic reversals when in railing against the king he now describes Richard as " that sweet lovely rose " and Bolingbroke as " this thorn, this canker ": and sitting there, listening to him, is that same silent, heavy Northumberland who was Bolingbroke's chief agent to the throne.

This interpretation of Harry Hotspur is rounded out in the subsequent "scenes from provincial life." The first of these, in his own castle with his wife, was produced to emphasise to the full the altogether wilder rougher, less courtly strain in this not wholly likeable Hotspur. From the very beginning of the scene (the long speech from Lady Percy which opens, " Oh my good Lord, why are you thus alone,") the pair of them adopt the kind of violence of sexuality which is derived

45

from the text of the later part of the scene (" Out, you mad-headed ape . . . weasel . . . paraquito . . . I'll break thy little finger . . . ").   In the spirit of these words, a tone of violence which you would never find at the Court, she upbraids him, and with the same kind of violence he pushes her away, not gently rebuffing but violently rejecting what are in effect violent sexual overtures, merging into a reconciliation in the closing passage.

This mood is picked up again in Act III, both in Hotspur's provoking of Owen Glendower, and in his love passages — with the same violent streak in them — with his wife.   In these ways a conception of Harry Hotspur is built up which remains true to all we hear of him — the sort of young man whose fiery spirit all the young might wish to emulate; but by a careful balancing of the traits it is conveyed as a character which, for all its good points, sits just that little bit lower than Hal's — or at least what Hal's, we already feel, potentially may become.   We have to feel — this is the point — that when it comes to the duel, we want Hal, not Harry, to win; and yet we mustn't, of course, feel for Harry Hotspur less than admiration.

In this production it was a triumph alike for producers and actor to have caught this delicate balance to a hair's breadth. In Mr. Michael Redgrave's Hotspur there was spirit to the highest degree — in his impatience he could hardly ever come down off the balls of his feet; yet in that very spirit there was just this unamiable excess of pride.   There was a rough violence of humour that was genuinely comic; but it brought up also the faintest whiff of the crude that fell short of real nobility. There was a virility and vitality and attack which raised the blood; but it was somehow just a little too self-interested, just a shade ego-maniacal.

Yet even to this Hal seems to have — in the short run at

46

least — a rather poor hand to offer. His qualities are all in bud. We shan't, until Part II, begin to see them flower and, if it is true that the great advantage of this presentation is that we can afford to wait, all the same if the flowering is to be really convincing, we must be adequately prepared for it. Somehow from the very first we must guess at the Hal who is to become Henry V. It isn't enough to know that he will. We must see that he will.

Mr. Richard Burton's intense withdrawn personality sets this conception off on just the right foot. He is an actor whose mere presence suggests depths of secret life behind the outward actions. His eyes have the far-away look of a young man whose inner life may be much more important than his outer. And this serves at once to set up a doubt in the audience's mind, a doubt — or rather a hope — that this Hal we are first of all shown is not by any means the whole person. His first scenes, after all, disclose a behaviour which is at odds with any idea of the perfect king he is to become; there are only two overt indications in Part I (his monologue to the audience, " I know you all and will a while behold . . . " and his scene with Bolingbroke) that he is going to turn out other than the reckless young scamp which shows on the surface. A reckless young scamp, that roughly is how the part is commonly played, a young man whose follies are the product of an excess of high spirits. But that would hardly do here, for the hero would find himself in the first part eclipsed by Harry Hotspur, while his long development would be both uninteresting and unconvincing.

Mr. Burton, by sheer virtue of his personality, was able to imply depths behind the shallowness. His behaviour is that of a young man indulging in his follies: but the inner life is altogether different. What it is, only becomes apparent as the cycle unrolls itself. For the moment it is enough that we see

47

that there is this inner, and more important, life and that it will develop along lines very different from his present behaviour.

Prince Hal's development is traced principally in relation to two characters, to Falstaff and to his father, Bolingbroke. His relation with Falstaff is established here with quite a distinct difference of emphasis from the usual. He is not the unselfconscious drinking companion of the customary production. When he looks at Falstaff, it is not with the connivance of a fellow conspirator. He looks at him from a distance, so to speak, a distance of reserve. And this reserve seems to disassociate him in part at least from the follies of Falstaff. This Prince Hal never seems to laugh *with* Falstaff, but always at him. He even holds off a little from the affection of such phrases as " My sweet beef, my sweet creature of bombast "; and though this may, at first hearing, strike an audience as cold (especially an audience accustomed to a real warmth between the two of them) it will pay off in the long run. For, in this presentation, it has to be remembered that we are playing straight up without a break to the rejection of Falstaff. That, when it comes, must be made perfectly acceptable.

So the sense of only a half participation must be established from the very beginning. When we first see them together, Hal comes in from above. It is one of those " mornings after the night before." He sluices his face in a bucket of water, and all the time he is cocking one ear. A great breathing and wheezing and snoring is coming from behind the curtain centre stage. It is Falstaff sleeping, and Hal wakes him up. Heaving himself out into the open, the old man stands there, twiddling his fingers while Hal rates him, " What a devil hast thou to do with the time of day?" On Falstaff's face is that sort of look you see on a favourite dog, accepting a scolding which it knows will not last. Yet Hal is quite unsmiling. Indeed we notice from the start about this Prince that there is

48

nothing between a perfectly straight face and a laugh bursting out, as if forced from him. He is constantly being wooed into laughter by the old ruffian and his verbal wit. Then see, how, under his laugh, Falstaff, eyeing him to watch the effect, rises to greater and greater extravagances. "Let us be Diana's foresters," he tries first, and seeing no response doubles it with "Gentleman of the shade; and, still getting no answer, reaches the perfect phrase "Minions of the moon" and, reaching it, how he coos it, and gets his laugh. This Prince is not an easy-hearted convivial boon-companion. He has to be lured into playing that role by extravagance. It is extravagance in any form that switches the Prince out of a sort of melancholy half-participation into a full-blooded one, as for instance again when Poins suggests that extra twist to the Gadshill expedition. Up to that point you feel that he might not have gone — or perhaps that he might. There's a sort of indifference, a pulling both ways that make for indifference, visible all the time in his slightly sullen look. By touches like these the end of this scene when he speaks out to the audience:

> " I know you all and will awhile behold
> The unyoked humour of your idleness "

comes as no sort of surprise. It doesn't pull us up: it springs from a side of his nature we have already been given a clear indication of.

Following this up there was one particularly notable piece of production which admirably succeeded in throwing our minds dramatically forward to the climax of Hal's development. It comes in Act II, Scene 4, the scene where Falstaff and Hal, turn by turn, play at being the king. We are warned of its coming just before they begin this game, when Falstaff apostophrises Hal:

> "But tell me, Hal, art thou not horribly afeard? Thou, being heir apparent, could the world pick thee out three such

49

enemies again as that fiend Douglas, that spirit Percy, and that devil Glendower? Art thou not horribly afraid? Doth not thy blood thrill at it?"

The Prince's answer to that is not given in the same spirit at all. It stops the joking with a sudden turn to the serious, and holds the stage still for a moment:

" Not a whit i'faith: I lack some of thy instinct."

This little drop into the serious prepares us for the longer piece that is coming. The Prince, it will be remembered, has been summoned the next day before his father, and, prompted by that, they decide to enact the scene foolingly; Falstaff is lumbered up on to the table and sits on the throne there catechising the Prince. It is an uproariously comic scene. Then they decide to change places: Hal mounts the table and enacts his father and Falstaff pretends to be the Prince. And then, when Hal in the course of his examination comes mockingly to mention Falstaff — " There is a devil that haunts thee in the likeness of a fat old man . . ."— the serious note suddenly re-appears. The accusations come unsmiling from that deadpan face, and, as they unwind, an uneasy feeling falls on the company and freezes their laughter. The equivocal feeling mounts to a tension as they reach Falstaff's, " My Lord, the man I know "; and explodes into a moment's queer, horrid silence at the Prince's accusation (it now amounts to that), " I know thou dost." There it is held for a moment until Falstaff pulls them all back into laughter by launching out in his own defence.

Played in this way, the scene has a very potent effect in dividing these two from one another in our sympathies. The division, which from now on grows between them, will after this seem not merely acceptable but inevitable. By Part II, of course, the danger (the danger of the Falstaff-Hal relationship becoming sentimentalised) has passed. Falstaff and Hal

50

Opposite. " For you my staff of office did I break In Richard's time." Worcester and Vernon (right) come to parley with the king.

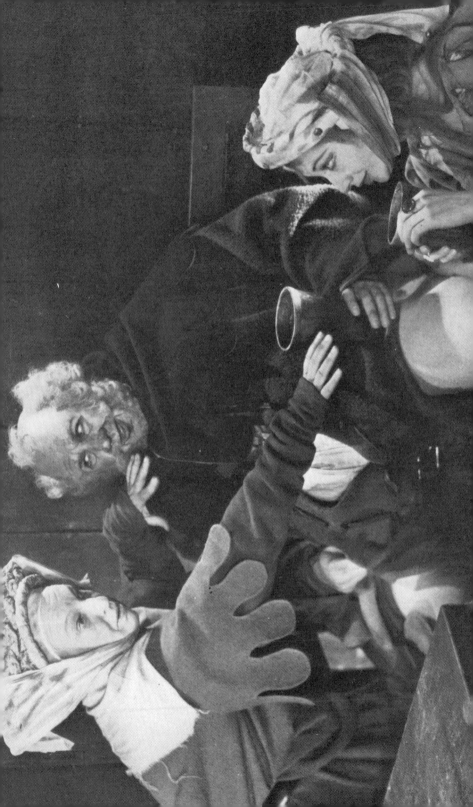

go more or less their own ways, and the Prince becomes for Falstaff little more in effect than a boasting point. There only remains the " rejection " scene, and by now we are ready for the shift of emphasis with which this must be played. It is usual for Falstaff to play this scene for its full pathos, and it is difficult not to let the new king's speech to him seem brutal and priggish. The effect is softened here partly by there never having been so close an affection between them as is commonly displayed, and by the division between them having been carefully established; partly by the actor (Mr. Quayle himself) deliberately and unselfishly playing the scene down as a sentimental scene, and playing up instead the fact that he feels publicly let down after all his bragging to Shallow, and quickly pulling his wits together (as in the play-acting scene above) and putting on a brave show.

The diminished effect of this scene has also been built up in advance from the angle of the other main participant. Hal himself has in the meantime been growing up to regality. For it is a different Hal we see when he is away from Falstaff. Or rather we see in the scenes with his father more clearly what is going on behind those eyes, when he is half listening to Falstaff's fun. In the first encounter with Bolingbroke Mr. Burton indicates a different version of the character from the usual. The far-away look seemed to be focussed more distinctly on an objective, on his future, on his destiny. There was no submissiveness, no air of being chastened, only a genuine contrition that he had caused the father he admires so much grief. What is hinted at, in short, is a more complicated relationship between this father and son than usual. This father is noble, generous, slow and above all direct. This son is deep, reserved, assured but essentially complex. He knows where, in the long run, he is going — that is the impression he gives us above all. But he can't explain him-

51

Opposite. " You are the weaker vessel as they say, the emptier vessel."
Mistress Quickly makes the peace between Falstaff and Doll Tearsheet.

self to this father. It is natural that his father should so mis-judge the situation as to compare his son to Richard in youth. Natural, too, that this son should not excuse himself but only assert in a ringing tone what he knows to be true of himself and his future.

The same misunderstanding lies between them even on the king's deathbed; and the pathos of this scene is immeasurably heightened for us by our having seen in the Prince what this father, being the kind of man he is, never can, or could see — this complicated quality of heart that all the same does know its own purpose, and has shown itself to us from the first moment of our seeing him waking Falstaff at the beginning of the first part.

Where the particular force and interest of this presentation in cycle lies with regard to Hal's development is in the flowering of his character between the death of Bolingbroke and Henry V. The long scene of the dying king, the endearing speech to his brothers who have evidently been affected with Bolingbroke's suspicions, the magnaminous treatment of the Lord Chief Justice — it is these scenes which bridge the passage from Eastcheap to the Throne, and which modify our view of the hero king. The production of *Henry V* is not essentially different when it is played in the cycle than what it would be at any other time. But the attitude of the audience towards the king undergoes a considerable modification. The young king who sits on that spotlighted throne where the light has played successively on Richard and on Bolingbroke is revealed in more dimensions than is commonly the case.

THE PRODUCTIONS
AND THEIR RECEPTION

WITHIN THE general conception, the individual productions were entrusted to different hands. Mr. Anthony Quayle produced the *Richard II*; for the *Henry IV* Part I, where he was himself playing Falstaff, he was assisted by Mr. John Kidd. Part II was produced by Mr. Michael Redgrave, and Mr. Quayle resumed again for *Henry V*.

In the account of these productions which follows, it must be remembered that, though the plays were planned as a cycle, they were presented, necessarily, play by play, at intervals, throughout the season: for each could only come into the repertory after a month or so to give its predecessor time to settle down. This meant that only two thirds way through the season was it possible to see the four plays straight off in succession; and only when they were so seen did they make their full impact as a unity.

The critics who came to the first nights at monthly intervals naturally tended to view the plays as separate entities and to judge the productions by the standards of individual presentation as they knew it in the past. A good many of the strictures passed were not in fact quite fair to this different way of presenting the plays. This was a trap into which I fell myself at the outset and one, consequently, that I have some sympathy for.

But before we go on to consider each play separately it may be as well to notice first the reception accorded to Miss Moiseiwitsch's set. This, as I have said, remained the same for all four plays. And it struck most people at first sight as rather chilling. In my first notice I said of it:

" A dark wooden platform raised on what is no more solid than, and not much different from, scaffolding, is mounted in the centre of the stage, with steps curving round each side of it. Its centre can be closed with dark wooden doors or can be left open to reveal more scaffold poles planted in barrels behind. It all has an air of improvisation, as of having been left half finished out of doors (so it works

53

rather badly against the indoors scenes). This contraption — for it looks like that — faces us when we come into the theatre, for this is one of those " No Curtain " productions; and it is to face us, I understand, unchanged, throughout this historical cycle. This is rather a daunting prospect. But it may well be that it will prove more suitable for the other plays than this one which differs from them considerably in character and feeling."

This set certainly proved efficient for passing the scenes quickly one after the other, but the erection was (necessarily on this stage) set rather far back; and this rather neutralised the intended Elizabethan effect. Mr. Ivor Brown in *The Observer* made this point:

" My eye was distracted by the great space behind the open doors and the curious array of poles set in barrels reaching back to the cyclorama. Shakespeare's stage was well boxed in; actor and audience shared a close confinement. Stratford's auditorium has been enormously improved, though not in appearance, by enlarging the dress circle so as to abolish cold wall spaces. The audience is at grips with the actors as never before, but the actors are handicapped by this visible vastness behind them."

Those barrels to which we both objected were subsequently removed, but even that did not reconcile many critics to the forbidding appearance of the set, although it was generally accepted that the idea in itself was a happy one. Mr. T. C. Kemp in *The Birmingham Post* said:

" The setting by Tanya Moiseiwitsch is an affair of stairways, platforms and galleries, constructed in rough timber and hinting at an Elizabethan theatre background. As in this artist's designs for *Henry VIII*, the playing space is restricted to odd landings, and the scene has the appearance

54

of a crossways between apartments. Any sense of royal occasion is blunted when affairs of State are conducted on the stairs. This scaffold is not easy on the players who are always either ascending or descending and do most of their business in the lobby."

But against these criticisms I should like to quote a letter which appeared in the *Sunday Times* signed Rosemary Anne Sisson, towards the end of the season, which received some support:

" This year at Stratford (for the first time as far as I know) there has been a real attempt to stage the history plays as Shakespeare intended them to be staged, while avoiding any painful sense of pedantic archaism. Tanya Moiseiwitsch's permanent set was not a reconstruction of the Globe Theatre, but an improvement on it. By using steps up to a wide gallery with doors opening out underneath it, the set had all the variety of Upper, Lower, and Inner Stage which the plays demand, but without the limitation of movement between, which was obviously an undesirable feature of the Globe."

As far as the mechanics are concerned I agree with this judgement. But I think that the set might well have been made more pleasing to the eye without any sacrifice of utility. On the other hand there was very general praise for Miss Moiseiwitsch's magnificent costumes, which certainly glowed richly against the plain background. And it must also be said that the set was less well suited to *Richard II* where it was first seen and judged than to the other three plays. Those who read on will see that it increasingly won respect, if not often affection, from those who came to see it regularly.

RICHARD II

THE OPENING night of a big season like this one is always fraught with difficulties, many of the kind which will be smoothed out as a production settles down. *Richard II* was no exception. To other first night accidents was added that Mr. Michael Redgrave broke a toe at the dress rehearsal and played the first night in great pain. But, accidents apart, what mainly contributed, in my view, to a rather cool critical reception of this first play was that the over-all conception was not at this stage clear in anyone's mind, nor the shifts of emphasis which this required from the actor playing Richard. What most of the experienced among the audience were, consciously or unconsciously, doing was bringing to bear as a standard of comparison the incomparable performance that Mr. John Gielgud gave in the title role before the war. It was difficult for the memory not be be dazzled by this recollection, and hard to adjust the faculties to a less romantic conception. The proof of this lies in the fact that it was to the performance of Mr. Michael Redgrave as Richard in isolation, that the critics (myself included) tended primarily to address themselves. To begin with my own notice in *The New Statesman and Nation*:

" Mr. Redgrave is set to play his character in a sense *against* the production. The lyricism of his part, which distills the very essence of a sweet adolescent self pity, was overshadowed. Mr. Redgrave gives an extremely sensitive and lyric performance, and if it doesn't as it should absolutely engulf us, isn't this because the production was deliberately designed to see that it does not? And though I think I follow the reason for this — namely to unify the play with those that follow — I cannot feel it to be right. And it was certainly not satisfying."

Later, when I had seen the plays played in succession I was

56

to find a different and most interesting kind of satisfaction. Mr. Alan Dent in the *News Chronicle* noticed a discrepancy which is only resolved as we progress through the plays:

" Mr. Redgrave plays the King in a flamboyant, honey sweet way that matches his sartorial splendour. In the first act he draws the scornful, mocking and spoilt young king — the royal playboy surrounded by his flattering yes-men — with a brilliant certainty.

In the later acts he seemed oddly deficient in pathos, and we found ourselves watching the excellent Bolingbroke instead of the King, for in this Bolingbroke's eye lurked an infinity of contemptuous patience while he heeded Richard's elaborately fanciful speeches."

The dramatic critic of *The Times* was also quick to see the Bolingbroke was no less important to this production than the Richard:

" The strictly theatrical pleasures of the opening night of the festival spring from two fine performances by Mr. Redgrave and Mr. Harry Andrews . . . Mr. Anthony Quayle has apparently directed on the assumption that all will be well so long as the contrast and conflict between Richard and Bolingbroke are thrown into powerful relief . . . Mr. Redgrave does not go out of his way to present Richard as the deliberate artist observing and exquisitely recording the processes of his own ruin. His Richard is, of course, a great deal of an artist and his delicate intuitions are sharpened by adversity: but in general the reading of the character suggests that a foppish trifler, as unpredictable and cruel as the most pampered coquette, becomes through the loss of his throne a man able, now that he is undistracted by temptation, to measure the world by a new standard. In the scene of his deposition this Richard is spiritually triumphant, so much so that the rest of the performance somehow declines in interest and the expected pathos of the prison scene scarcely appears."

Mr. Ivor Brown in *The Observer* dissented from the last part of this judgement:

"Richard is reflective not rhetorical, a poet philosopher who handles a conceit more subtly than ever he did the sceptre. His luxurious self-indulgence needs colour all about him and, though he has been beautifully robed, and the lighting set moves rythmically to his aid, he is hindered by the dun look of the background. Michael Redgrave plays the part finely; the early scenes of careless time-fleeting in his golden days among the degenerate favourites are most vivid, and I found no lack of poignancy in the hours of decline and doom."

Mr. Peter Fleming in *The Spectator* feels that the early scenes were successful at the expense of the later:

"Richard (who at the end kills two of his assassins with their own weapons) should always be formidable . . . even when the King is down he should still have the power to awe or anyhow to disconcert; it should still seem natural to address him as "redoubted sir" and there should be an uneasy stirring, a feeling of "what the devil is he up to now" when Richard sends for a mirror. All this Mr. Redgrave abjures, giving us instead a poised and finished portrait of a sad, poetical, dilettante in whom the loss of his throne occasions the same wistful, reflective melancholy as the loss of his horse, and whose seat on both one suspects to have been equally unprofessional. It is a performance with many moments of grace and beauty, but it is not (to me at any rate) a very satisfying performance."

G.F. in *The Manchester Guardian* found an odd contradiction

58

Opposite. "Thou bring'st me happiness and peace, Son John;
But health alack with youthful wings is flown
From this bare withered trunk . . ."
The dying Henry Bolingbroke with his sons.

in the interpretation (a contradiction, once again which is deliberately emphasised here for the purpose of the cycle as a whole):

" Michael Redgrave, in effect, plays two kings. One, dressed in what fashion writers call pastel shades, shrugs and turns his head and gives slashing feminine glances with his pale blue eyes as he fingers a weak chin and hopelessly tries to keep order among his squabbling courtiers. The second speaks and carries himself more manfully and dresses more soberly. The whole character, as Mr. Redgrave sees it, is a nervous emotional incompetent who undervalues his crown while he wears it, gives it up without a fight when Bolingbroke raises his voice, and then bitterly regrets his weakness. Later in the season these three aspects of the man will no doubt be put together with fewer obvious seams than there were last night."

Those who were lucky enough to see later productions of the play found that Mr. Redgrave had already modified the extravagances of the opening scenes. Mr. Richard Findlater in *Tribune* who saw a later performance, as well as the first, noted:

" On the first night, Mr. Redgrave gave a fine performance which somehow failed to make any impact. His Richard, as many critics have observed, is in two halves. As the Royal umpire of the opening scenes Richard appears as a dainty feline homosexual, purring with malice and affection: on his return from Ireland he has suffered a sea change into something much less rich and strange, a melancholy noble prince making phrases out of his own disasters. It is a transformation scene which Mr. Redgrave made neither credible nor comfortable. Moreover in spite of a scrupulous care for balance of phrase and meaning of words, he fell into

59

Opposite. " Fill the cup and let it come
I'll pledge you a mile to the bottom."
Master Silence sings in Justice Shallow's orchard.

the bad habit of imposing on the verse a quavering drone of spurious poetic intensity which by its humming monotony lulls the speech into a common grave.

At the first matinée Mr. Redgrave gave a wonderful performance: one not only admired it from a distance but felt it on the pulse . . . the irrelevant incantations had disappeared, and Mr. Redgrave spoke throughout with fine precision and careful melody, marking the rhyme stresses with a light insistence. He also modified the effeminacy of the early Richard, and though one missed the memorable exaggerations of the first night it gave the character more unity."

Mr. Harold Hobson who saw the production late in the season payed Mr. Redgrave's Richard this tribute in the *Sunday Times*:

" The surprising feature of Mr. Redgrave's Richard was that this actor, after both Mr. Geilgud and Mr. Guinness had reaped the field before him, found it possible to come home with his arms full of sheaves that his eminent predecessors had over-looked. Whether Mr. Redgrave discovered anything so moving as Mr. Geilgud's luxuriant self-pity or Mr. Guinness' beautiful exercises in spontaneous poetry may be debated. I myself think not. But he certainly gave us a Richard consistent in himself, in one respect more credible than any we have seen before, and quite new.

The briefest way of expressing the original quality of Mr. Redgrave's performance is to say that this is the only Richard I have ever seen who could conceivably have suppressed Wat Tyler's rebellion . . . Mr. Gielgud offered us a Richard who would have met the rebellion with adolescent tears, Mr. Guinness a Richard who would have met it with adolescent verses. Mr. Redgrave's Richard, on the other hand would have met and overcome it, with strong adolescent nerves.

Mr. Quayle's production, was clear, direct and swift though there were some who thought that it sagged a little in the later part. One criticism was generally voiced, namely his treatment of York. *The Times* remarked:

" York, so sorely divided between his horror of spilling the blood of an anointed King and his recognition of the Kinglike qualities of the Usurper represents the political dilemma of the time. Mr. Quayle causes Michael Gwynn to play the important Duke as a wander-witted dotard, and for a mere trifle in the way of comic relief barters a vital element in the drama."

And though Mr. Ivor Brown again dissented: " Michael Gwynn that constantly exciting actor, gives a new and amusing humanity to the palsied Duke of York, breaking the verse to a jerky prose, but making a fresh arresting figure of that embarrassed neutral in baronial conflict "— the sense of the meeting was against him.

Certainly there is a case for York's neutralism getting one or two laughs. But this is not quite the same as playing him as a comic character as Mr. Gwynn did. His actions may on occasions have been comic but his dilemma is a real and serious one. To quote myself:

" York is not a kind of Vicar of Bray; he believes in order. The divine right of Kings which Richard embodies is the principle of order on which he has been brought up. But in Richard's person it has produced only disorder. Bolingbroke is a traitor to this principle of order, and yet in his person he does embody order. That is the dilemma of York. And it is by no means a joke."

Mr. Gwynn is a loyal and sound actor, but on this occasion

61

he seems to have stood a little outside his part, commenting as it were, on his own behaviour. And the producer not only allowed but evidently encouraged him, if we may take as evidence one piece of business. When Bolingbroke on his arrival in the country, comes to Berkeley Castle and finds York in possession, York finally — and admittedly the action has a touch of comedy in it — invites him and his followers to stay the night. Bolingbroke accepts the offer and passes in. Northumberland is following close behind, but York pertly steps between them and demands precedence, pushing Northumberland out of the way. The manner in which this was done was quite frankly low comedy.

The one other general criticism I have was that Richard's young entourage overdid the emotion. They howled and writhed and wept altogether too much, and that not only in the moment of defeat and the fear of death, but before it too. These two misjudgements stood out particularly sharply just because the rest of the production was so particularly faithful and dramatic. I remember that this fact struck the members of " The Critics " team from the B.B.C. very favourably when we visited *Richard II* in the middle of its run. We kept remarking upon small effective points of production: how impressively and pointedly, for instance, contrasts were established in the opening scenes of the quarrels between the nobles: how extraordinarily effective just before Richard's entry in the deposition scene was the proclamation of Henry IV, and Bolingbroke's noble stalk up to the throne when he assumes it, with a trace all the same of a not untroubled defiance of the future. Indeed it seemed to us that the production was full of imaginative and really helpful touches which brought out the contrasts and created the atmosphere, not wilfully or exotically, but out of the text itself.

The major part which Bolingbroke has to play in the series

62

Opposite. " Die men like dogs. Have we not Hiren yet? "
Doll, Falstaff, Pistol, Mistress Quickly, Bardolph and
the page, at the Boar's Head Tavern.

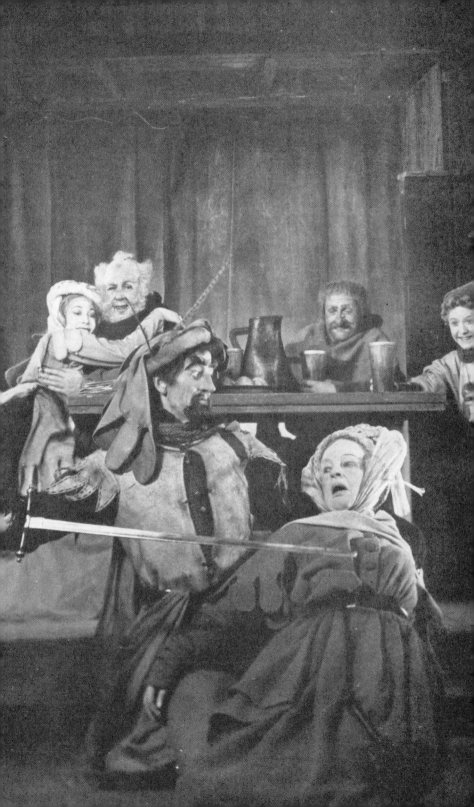

does not fully make itself felt in the first play. But already Mr. Harry Andrews had begun the process of establishing him in the centre of the picture. *The Spectator* described his performance as being " as good as it could have been;" and Mr. Eric Keown of *Punch* said that Mr. Andrews " made Bolingbroke tremendously full of natural authority, nothing in it better than his surly slightly uncomfortable reception, glooming on the throne, of Richard's abdication." *The Manchester Guardian* underlined this in remarking that: " the vigour and flamboyance of Mr. Andrews' Bolingbroke promises that he will be a wonderful Henry IV. When, in the end, he lounges attentively on the throne and glowers contemptuously at the abdicating Richard, his eyes say many things which are only hinted at in the text."

The subsidiary roles were particularly well filled. Foremost among them I should place Mr. Alexander Gauge's portrait of Northumberland. I have already indicated the importance of this role in the general conception, and Mr. Gauge's version of it must, like Harry Andrews' Bolingbroke, have delighted Mr. Quayle by its faithfulness to his idea. It was perfect casting, of course, in the first place. Mr. Gauge's large solid block of a figure, his bull neck and heavy head, were just what was wanted; he made a deep impression just with that, standing granite-like, unshakable, unspeaking, during the early scenes; and then when he spoke, Mr. Gauge added a note which perfectly revealed his character. It is hard to describe. It was a form of arrogant disdain noticeable in the proud — a sort of peeling off of his phrases as if he were handling something objectionable to the smell, and keeping it away from his nose. Actually he has some fine phrases to speak, but he seemed to be saying them with a sort of self-amused contempt, as if to imply " I too can do this kind of thing if it's what is wanted." " Haut," indeed, Mr. Gauge

63

Opposite. " God save thy Grace. King Hal! My Royal Hal."
The coronation procession just before the rejection scene
(c.f. plate 10)

showed himself and "Insulting," too, but with the subtlest kind of insult, that which hurts all the more for being coolly planted.

Mr. Hugh Griffith received many epithets of praise for his Gaunt " A welsh projection " as *The Times* remarked " quite acceptable since Mr. Griffith rightly insists on acting a part which others have often been tempted to declaim." But this was not ideal casting and Mr. Griffith seemed to me to display a dangerous tendency to drop the end of his lines into inaudibility. His last quarrel with the King was very finely done. I have never seen this scene so well produced, with such beautifully stepped up climaxes. Mr. William Fox's Mowbray was another particularly well sketched minor character; a really passionate intensity informed him so that one felt the absolute conviction of the man. Mr. Basil Hoskins made something real of the equivocal Aumerle, a pleasing sprig too easily swayed. Mr. Robert Hardy anticipated Mr. Redgrave's Doric and his attack in the next play, while Mr. Duncan Lamont spoke up movingly and powerfully for Richard in the deposition scene, and Mr. William Squire made a farouche Piers Exton.

The women get little chance in these historical plays, but Richard's queen has a small opportunity which Miss Heather Stannard, as I thought, did not quite discover in the part. Somehow she remained resolutely out of period and there is some trick of her face which made even her sad looks seem touched with a smile. "Richard's not very sad Queen," *The Times* described her. But Mr. Harold Hobson, for one, found more in her than that — " Miss Heather Stannard's Queen, foreseeing disaster where others as yet perceive only gaiety, was a touching performance." As throughout the plays the crowd were admirably disciplined and effectively arranged and the stage management — no small matter in these large-scale productions — exemplary.

HENRY IV PART I

THE *Henry IV* Part I struck me and many other observers, as being far away the most consistent production of the four. Indeed it was quite the best production of the play I remember seeing. I find it a little hard on recollection to state exactly why. I can think of a number of things, for instance, that didn't quite come off. The robbery on Gadshill for one, was decidely jumbled and hurried, and the very difficult battle scene before Hotspur and Hal's duel did not succeed. But overriding any details was a smoothness and a pace which carried the play unfaltering through from start to finish. The critic in *Truth* found the production " absorbingly good ":

" From the start the action gets into its stride; characterisation manages to be conscientious without being conventional; the economically rapid changes of scene go hand in hand with the requisite variation of mood and *tempo* without loss of time. The result, delineated more forcefully than I can remember in past presentations, is the first half of a dramatic panorama representing the turbulent reign of Bolingbroke, a man who, with all his faults, honestly felt himself called upon to assume power to the extent of seizing it."

Mr. T. A. Jackson in the *Daily Worker* underlined this point:

" Let me say at once that the performance was very fine. The stage setting reproduced admirably the lay-out of the stage of Shakespeare's day and so made possible all the pageantry business without any of that over lavish gorgeousness deemed imperative on the flat stage of Beerbohm Tree and Henry Irving. The pageantry and grouping were well designed and perfectly rehearsed; the actors played as a team—nobody trying to steal the picture from anybody else."

65

And Mr. Brian Harvey wrote in the *Birmingham Gazette*:

" This is a rich, bustling Shakespeare — full of colour and vigour. It thrusts on with spirit, energy, pace and lusty enjoyment of its tavern humours and its political insurrection. What a rich pageantry all this forms."

By now, too, we were beginning to see how the design would work out. I wrote of this production in *The New Statesman*:

" It is an unqualified success: swift, exciting, varied, excellently produced, and well acted throughout, and we begin to see, too, the force of playing these four plays in a cycle with continuity of actors and production. It is, historically, a help to have the events of *Richard II* so alive in our memories, and, no less, we have to look forward to the events that are coming and trim present sails to fit future scenes. One may almost see the producer's mind ranging forwards and backwards from this point. For instance, there is a prime difficulty ahead for a present day audience, namely the priggish dismissal of Falstaff by Prince Hal; and then, when we have swallowed that, there is a further obstacle, the Prince, with his priggishness fresh in our minds, has to be transformed into the perfect flower of chivalry in Henry V. Already Mr. Quayle is working on us to put us into the state where we have sensed what is to follow."

By " Mr. Quayle " in this context, I meant to represent him in both capacities, as producer and as the actor of Falstaff. Many people found a certain lack of warmth in his portrait and the dramatic critic of *The Times* understood why:

" Prince Hal seems scarcely to enjoy Falstaff and rarely brings himself to bandy base comparisons with the rascal without introducing a covert threat. The Falstaff of Mr. Anthony Quayle is more than half aware that his standing

66

Opposite. " A' made a finer end, and went away, an it had been any christom child . . ." Falstaff's death rehearsed by Pistol, Mistress Quickly, Nym, Francis, Bardolph.

with the Prince is in doubt. This awareness has affected his geniality, for Mr. Quayle is strictly loyal to the Festival's historical design. His make-up is rather grotesque than laughable; he speaks the jests with metallic precision; and his smile when it appears is a painted smile. This tuned-down Falstaff has the supreme merit of suiting the production, and no one but a very good actor could bring it off half so well."

The critic of *The Manchester Guardian* took a rather idiosyncratic view:

"Anthony Quayle's own Falstaff has become fundamentally careworn; he seems supremely conscious of his own depravity. One has an awestruck feeling that beneath the padded belly, the swollen legs and the slightly too clownish pink and white paint on the face, modernity is gnawing at a pathological Fat Knight. He is not food for powder but for case-books and clinics, a sick man who brags, but not as though he believes in his own bluster. Even Richard Burton's Prince Hal seems to have the patient under observation. The text gives room for this reading, but it is not a gay one and it forswears gusto. It makes one think but it does not make one merry."

Too high a pitch in his voice, and too little drink in it, was a common criticism. Mr. Ivor Brown described it:

"A tenor-voiced monster, with a nice turn of philosophy which he flutes to us in his private meditations. The gross humour, though given with skill and relish does not overlay the wit."

But it must not be forgotten that Mr. Quayle's Falstaff was played for a purpose. To continue my own notice:

"His own Falstaff is never for a moment sentimentalised. It never counts on his own ideal reputation, on the affection

67

Opposite. "If we may pass, we will, if we be hindered
We shall your tawny ground with your red blood
Discolour . . " Harry receives the French Herald, Montjoy.

he has won in the past to insinuate himself into our sympathy
. . . Mr. Quayle refuses every chance of making any claim on
our sentiment. He is superbly funny but openly con-
temptible; thus we shall not have in due course more than a
parting pang for the treatment of this Falstaff."

But I think that the coolness necessary for this conception
resulted in Mr. Quayle's Falstaff being rather undervalued.
Mr. Quayle seemed to me to get to perfection two aspects of
the part. First, he had a wonderful relish in the phrases, a
really pleasurable folding of the tongue and teeth about the
language itself. Then again Mr. Quayle caught exactly the
right tone (for this production in cycle) of a favourite jester
who is never quite certain of his master's moods; who must
expect a whipping now and again though he is confident of
being forgiven in the end; but who, out of his master's sight
was as bold a braggart as ever boasted. These points were
better appreciated in the second part, when the presence of
a rather unusually cold Hal was less in evidence.

Mr. Richard Burton as Prince Hal had to support this reading
from the other side. The coldness in fact came from him, and
that coldness comes from his sense of his own destiny. Mr.
Harold Hobson in the *Sunday Times* paid a glowing tribute to
this aspect of Mr. Burton's performance:

   " The suggestion of greatness (which Mr. Burton displayed) is not a thing of flashes merely, coming only at the
   crisis of the play, though that in itself would be sufficiently
   memorable. It is in the bone and sinew of the performance,
   and is as evident in the actor's stillness when other players
   are speaking as when he is sailing the full flood . . . Through
   the gaiety and noise and lechery through which he chose to
   move (Mr. Burton) carried a quiet face whose repose was a
   constant dumb rebuke. This face, which is not without a

touch of sullenness, is occasionally lit by a small smile of thoughtful radiance, and its eyes seem not quite of the earth. Mr. Burton looked like a man who had had a private vision of the Holy Grail, and was as determined to say nothing about it as he was incapable of forgetting it . . .Instead of a lighthearted rapscallion Mr. Burton offers a young knight keeping a long vigil in the cathedral of his own mind. The Knighthood is authentic, the vigil upheld by interior exaltation."

Mr. Ivor Brown discerned the same traits:

" An excellent feature of this production is the emphasis on Prince Hal's sense of destiny. The madcap side of him, sometimes overstressed, is played down: Richard Burton's admirable performance is one of every-inch-a-King-to-be. He can sport with Falstaff, but he knows the old rake's limitations, and the rejection of him in Part II will thus be more natural than if both had been larking on equal terms. The idea that there is a ' problem ' in Hal's attitude to Falstaff fades away when the Prince's part is thus clearly conceived and firmly executed. Mr. Burton is not just a play-boy turned swordsman in the final fight with Hotspur, which the latter so inexplicably loses if the Prince is only a capering lightweight. He is the future Henry of Agincourt, emerging from the clouds of dissipation whence, as he carefully explains, he will emerge sun-like."

It was in this play that the stature of Mr. Harry Andrews' portrait of Henry Bolingbroke began to make itself felt. It is partly due to the grandeur of his performance, the critic in *The Times* suggests, that the historical design is "not upset by the intractably comic figure of Falstaff :

" Mr. Harry Andrews plays Henry IV with a concentrated vigour which brings tinglingly alive the man who is efficient enough to usurp a Kingdom but lacks the imagination to rule it. While Mr. Andrews is on the stage there is no fear that the play will surrender its dynamic unity of Royal history to the static unity of a pervading humorous personality."

The critic in *Truth* writes:

" Harry Andrews conveys the fundamental patriot, not without remorse at his own ruthless advent to a throne, but resolved to be King who, at all costs, must rule. Those who are not with him are against him, and their point of view is not to be weighed against his demand for their unqualified loyalty. The actor's vigour and attack stand him in good stead in the first clash with Hotspur, and never relax."

And Miss Siriol Hugh Jones summed up in *Vogue* what every critic felt about this fine performance:

" As for Harry Andrews' King Henry, the pivot-point and corner stone of the whole edifice, rarely has there been seen a more heroic, splendid portrait, finely spoken, noble to the eye and most movingly developed from powerful youth to haunted old age."

Mr. Harry Andrews made the deep slow character of the King ripe with dignity and weight. This King as we compared him in our minds with Richard was a Lion in person as well as in title, an ageing Lion in a rage. I remember particularly, for instance, how brilliantly conducted was the second scene with Northumberland and Worcester. Worcester's genuine feeling of grievance, Northumberland's disdainful temper, and riding above them the King's air of absolute authority, expressed in the perfectly phrased outburst of autocratic ill-temper when, having dismissed Worcester, he turns to Northumberland with " You / were / about /

70

to / speak." And, I remember, following on that, the noble dignity of his reproof to his son.

Mr. Michael Redgrave took the part of Hotspur in this play, and it is a great credit to his unselfishness that he refrained from spoiling the design by "stealing the play." That he should not do so was implicit, of course, in the conception. All the same, his Hotspur was not unjustly described by the critic in *Punch* as:

"The best thing he has done. It is impetuous, charming and naive at the same time, and the stammer is omitted for a very difficult dialect which they say is Northumbrian."

The critic in *Truth* observes that:

"Mr. Michael Redgrave's Hotspur gives balance to the play by underlining a temperamental contrast. A soldier whose sense of honour smarts under a sense of royal injustice to a friend, he is, at the same time, a man with a sense of humour, a quality entirely lacking in his impatient liege. It is an unorthodox Hotspur, who misses no chance for dry sarcasm even at the fateful crossroads of allegiance."

Let me sum up the chorus of praise with an extract from my own review:

"His Hotspur is a most vivid characterisation of the impetuous, ardent young soldier, whose words tumble over each other in their impatience to get themselves out, who is always on the edge of action, even in repose, perpetually balanced up on the balls of his feet ready to spring, all of a straight supple piece. A brilliant dynamic performance."

The Falstaffian crew were well cast and played. Mr. Alan Badel was a fine-boned, quick-witted Poins who made an excellent bridge between Falstaff and the reserved Prince. Mr. Michael Bates was as bandy legged and bottle-nosed a Bardolph as anyone could wish for, while Miss Rosalind

71

Atkinson's unflagging energy brought Mistress Quickly very well into the picture.

It is particularly important in these large scale productions that the minor roles should be played with an unostentatious skill. From the ageing King's court we want only dignity and the feeling of affectionate respect that he inspires in his followers; Jack Gwillim and Raymond Westwell provided just this as Westmorland and Blunt. Among the rebels several critics noticed how Mr. William Fox's sincerity came in very tellingly for the not quite whole-hearted Vernon, and Mr. Duncan Lamont's presence and voice spoke well for the angry Worcester. Mr. Hugh Griffith was the obvious Glendower and perhaps a little over-indulged himself in enjoying the role. Miss Barbara Jefford as Lady Percy without having the accent to match Hotspur matched him anyhow in spirit. And, indeed, taken all round there was no one to let down the very high level of performance.

HENRY IV PART II

HENRY IV PART II is by common consent less well put together by its author than Part I. It is more rambling and episodic; and our interest has rather run down in the political events. That, at any rate is what one feels when one sees the play presented on its own. In that case Falstaff rules supreme, and one sits with what patience one can through most of the scenes from which he is absent. As a consequence, this is the play that has most to gain from the presentation in cycle. Enough excitement has been generated earlier in the plots and counter-plots to keep the interest still flickering; while the great scenes of Henry IV's death gain immeasurably from our having traced the relationship of father and son from its beginning. As observers were quick to notice, when Part II takes its place in the tetralogy, Falstaff is brought into a proper proportion and the other sides of the play " come up " appreciably.

Mr. Darlington in *The Daily Telegraph* put it like this:

" There is no doubt that in its place in this sequence *Henry IV* Part II becomes more important, because more comprehensible, than ever it can be when standing alone. By itself it is little more than the comedy of Falstaff, with a little tiresome historical stuff sticking in its edges. In the series, as we saw it tonight it becomes a piece of significant history, with a fine climax in Henry IVth's death scene played with emotion and strength by Harry Andrews as the King and Richard Burton as the Prince."

Mr. Michael Redgrave was responsible for the production which as *The Birmingham Mail* remarks:

" Was a presentation which though it was not so notable as Part I for its urgent sense of the immediate, or spiced so liberally with the recurrent excitement of surprise, was strongly buttressed with dramatic moments. It was the drama rather than the fooling that one best remembers. Harry Andrews, who has been proving so strong a fulcrum in this series, carried the aged, ailing King along his last troubled stretch with finely controlled dramatic power. There has, as yet in these histories never been a more finely acted scene than that between the dying King and Prince Hal."

Mr. Harry Andrews' performance was generally recognised as being the culmination of a really prodigious role. T.C.K. in *The Birmingham Post* sums it up:

" In the production by Michael Redgrave the dramatic scales were tipped heavily in favour of royalty chiefly by the playing of Harry Andrews as Henry. Mr. Andrews' performance throughout the three plays of the cycle has pro-

ceeded in a high curve which has encircled the Lancastrian
story with fine feeling. The calculated determination with
which Bolingbroke deposes Richard, the firm grasp of the
sceptre, the unease which grows when rebellion raises its
head, all these have been strongly recorded by Mr. Andrews.
Tonight he showed the King in decline and beautifully en-
compassed the tragedy of failing strength. Yet as the grasp
loosened on the uneasy sceptre, and the royal glance faded
from the eyes, the leonine head was occasionally lifted in
a hint of the old dominance."

The critic of *The Manchester Guardian* added his tribute to
the rest:

" The real heroic link of the first three plays of this ambitious sequence is the life and death of Bolingbroke transformed into King Henry. Harry Andrews carried the
epic story, fiery into grey, with unbroken power. Seldom
has approaching death been done with grimmer sincerity,
till failing strength has quenched even the flashing eye."

Even those who had been a little grudging over Mr. Quayle's
Falstaff impact in Part I, agreed with the general verdict that
his performance in this play excelled. Mr. Brian Harvey in
the *Birmingham Gazette* found that:

" Anthony Quayle gives us a much merrier and a mellower
Falstaff than he did at the opening of Part I. His characterisation has now developed a jovial impetus which urges
the portly man briskly through the play."

And Mr. Alan Dent was won over:

" Anthony Quayle's Falstaff still has the voice of a man
at least half his apparent age and weight. But, despite
this fundamental fault, it is a Falstaff that grows more endearing the more one sees and hears of it. He has a mis-
chievous twinkle in his roving old eyes, a wicked old smile

74

Opposite. " My Lord of Orleans, and my
lord high Constable, talk you of horse and armour?"
The French Camp; the Dauphin's tent.

playing over his round mouth, and the legs under the enormous paunch certainly look old in iniquity though they are preternaturally active for their age."

Mr. Cecil Wilson in the *Daily Mail* found that Falstaff:

" Has on the other hand grown younger with the years. His performance is sprightlier, more robust, and altogether better than before. His girth has not diminished but the gargoyle make-up has been toned down, giving his face and voice a proper chance to express themselves. The decrepit totter gives place to a gouty but vigorous limp, and the very vitality of the man makes his final deflation seem all the harsher."

Personally I did not find this difference in the two Falstaff's. T.C.K. in *The Birmingham Post* is nearer my own view:

" Anthony Quayle develops the knight along the lines of rascality, hauteur and artfulness which he laid down in Part I of the play, but the old man grows more vehement in villainy. Mr. Quayle makes no bones about the rascality. Falstaff's misdemeanours are not gentlemanly lapses though they are excused in aristocratic accents. They are the deliberate doings of one who knows he has a bad name and is determined to live up to it. Mr. Quayle's eulogy of Sherris-sack is delivered with the gusto of a vendor who believes in his wares."

The Manchester Guardian critic found that the charges he had laid in Part I no longer applied:

" Either Mr. Redgrave or Mr. Anthony Quayle himself has managed to draw Falstaff back from chronic invalidism . . . Mr. Quayle's Falstaff is now much lustier and less like what people's phrase would describe as " death warmed up " (a picture which in this production is achieved of set purpose by William Squires' Master Silence) Falstaff here storms out

75

Opposite. " I was not angry since I came to France Until this instant."
Fluellen carries the body of the boy before Hal.

the praise of Sack passage with rebellious gusto and if the old rascal has comic subtleties that are still uncaught, his portrait is better than it was."

Mr. Richard Burton is seen continuing his remarkable study of Prince Hal. *The Times* comments:

" Even in the comparatively carefree days of the Gadshill robbery, the Prince of Mr. Burton was a detached and rather critical participant in the frisk. Now, with the throne nearer his grasp, he is less often in Falstaff's company and on these occasions his detachment is complete. He relishes still the old man's wit, but treats any assumption of friendliness as so much pitch, examining it with a careful curiosity. Mr. Burton maintains this detachment with a hard smiling grace."

In the *Birmingham Gazette* Mr. Brian Harvey describes this performance as:

" A most moving and beautifully spoken portrait of a happy high spirited young man approaching both his own maturity and the responsibility of Kingship in a mood of boyish wonder and devotion."

The Manchester Guardian critic also felt the growth in the Prince:

" At certain earlier points Richard Burton as Prince Hal has just been a little lightened since Part I, but no one can complain 'I know thee not old man' is not achieved with sufficient severity. And why not? If the sober playboy is to turn dynastic and ungracious it is no use boggling about with compunction."

In this play the austere setting began to put on the decoration which flowered in Henry V.

" The closing scenes of public pageantry," remarks *The*

Manchester Guardian, " make striking use of crowds and colour; it was unexpected to see the basic dry wood of the Tanya Moiseiwitsch timbered setting blossom so abundantly into warmth. And in earlier scenes Mr. Redgrave softened that same asperity by glimpses of lighted interiors and of side booths and shops opened for London's traffic. It is a welcome touch and can help one to overlook too much stridency in the Tavern scene, though Rosalind Atkinson can still endow Mistress Quickly with a shrewish kick that seems not out of keeping."

The critic in *The Observer* drew attention to the merits of the small part playing:

" Throughout the comedy scenes were undertones of poignacy shadowed and mingled with the blaze of Bardolph's nose. Shallow himself is more than a ridiculous fribble; he is the shadow of all senile vanity, pomp strutting in an eel skin . . . Alan Badel, doubling Poins and Shallow proves a versatility which really asks for no proof, and turns the folly of the Justice to sweet, pathetic antics. Heather Stannard makes a brave termagant, but is too young to catch the maturity of a trollop who can remember death among the chambering and wantoning. Michael Gwynn's Chief Justice is admirable, Richard Wordsworth disproves my belief that Pistol is only a topical joke."

Mr. Philip Hope-Wallace was one of the first critics to sample the plays in cycle: he came to see the two Parts of *Henry IV* in succession and his criticism of the two of them together comes in aptly here:

" To see the two parts of Henry IV in one day, as I have just done is to enjoy the first really exciting Shakespearian acting of this year and to get, at last, a just view of this wonderful chronicle . . . I will not hestitate to say this is a

77

far better and more plausible production than the much praised Old Vic post-war world-tourer . . . Even character by character, it stands up to memories of that great team.

The general triumph of this production is to make good the study, as one thinks Shakespeare meant it, of Prince Hal's apprenticeship in Royalty, so that we see him growing before our eyes and know what must come at the end, not a ' priggish ' repudiation of Falstaff but a necessary step, indeed the sacrifice which we see Royalty exacting relentlessy from those worthy to assume it . . . Richard Burton, sturdy, Welsh, with a warmth and magnetism most unusual in so young an actor (heaven-sent qualities yet to be fully exploited), makes us accept this idea. It is a performance of great charm; into the wide set eyes, the wide face, we read only what is in our imagination, but what a gift thus to act as focus, as hearth for sympathy!

It is helped by the intelligent shaping and slanting of the play and particularly of Falstaff, whom finally, and more in Part II, I came to admire, unfailing in voice, in ' making the point ' . . . It was a long time before Mr. Quayle was getting through his disguise and communicating fully. But at the battle of Shrewsbury and again when aching with boredom in Shallow's garden he was very good indeed.

So was Shallow, Alan Badel, with Silence (William Squire) coming up excellently beside him — a wonderfully funny scene if rather over-produced . . . Of the other characters in this vast canvas I lack space to speak fully; Harry Andrews is excellent as King Henry, sonorous, grave, with severe eye, finally meeting death in the Jerusalem Chamber. Michael Bates's Bardolph, Barbara Jefford's Lady Percy and Hugh Griffith's Glendower stand out too among a lot of very excellent repertory playing. The particular glory of the first part, the best part, is Michael Redgrave's Hotspur . . .

78

Opposite. " What says she, fair one, that the tongues of men are full of deceits?" Harry's wooing.

what virtuosity, what richness of playing — and of communication, which I note specially, having missed just that in Mr. Redgrave's Hamlet recently. The detail, the variety and uninhibited flow were quite exceptional — the parting with Lady Percy (in all its implications) and the formidable exertions in the final throes were acting of the kind which holds up the breath in the spectator: the rare, the occasional thing."

HENRY V

BY THE TIME we reach Henry V the particular interest of the " presentation in cycle " is all but over. What we are left with is watching the young King whose development we have traced taking over the reins. Those of us who had been experiencing the cycle as a cycle knew what to expect of this Henry V — little in the way of heroics or rhetoric, much in the way of humanity and grace. Those, on the other hand, who " came in at the end " were looking for the customary schoolboy hero and tended to come in a " journalistic " spirit to see whether or not this new and exciting actor, Mr. Richard Burton, would provide it. So the reception of this play centred round the King's part and falls roughly into these two divisions, those who were following the cycle and those who came hoping to see, as Mr. Ivor Brown puts it, the Lewis Waller of the 1950's. The second party were, on the whole, disappointed.

Even so comparatively sober an organ as the *Sunday Times* caught something of the journalistic approach to the production. In the absence of the regular critic, Mr. Harold Hobson, Mr. J. W. Lambert told us:

" At Stratford last Tuesday one great question pervaded the town. The leaves on the riverside trees seemed to ask it, and the water reflected their enquiry; ancient houses raised gables like interrogating eyebrows, and hotel bars

79

Opposite. The set as it is transformed into the French palace for the final conference.

were loud with speculation. Would he bring it off? Could young Mr. Richard Burton, so compelling a Prince in *King Henry IV*, grow into Henry the hero, King and man in one?"

Mr. Lambert went on, in a perceptive notice, to prove himself one of the several who thought that he didn't quite:

" He is in many ways very fine; and if he does not quicken the blood, it is not merely because he seems rather short, or because, when volume is needed the voice becomes hard and monotonous. The real difficulty is that he is playing all the time against the spirit of Shakespeare's Henry . . . Perhaps the differences between young Prince Hal and the soldier King are too great to allow the two to be welded into one developing character. Mr. Burton does not in fact develop; he remains the sturdy, square-faced boy with a clipped skull cap of straight hair; he gives a purposeful severity to all his movements; he looks down a great deal, but often gazes straight out with the air of a man seeing visions, or glints sideways out of eyes suddenly narrowed and beady.

Thus he invests his Henry with that curious air of combined spirituality and cunning which looks out from so many early Italian paintings. He gives in fact an impression wholly Mediæval in spirit of a character wholly Renaissance in conception."

Lack of height (" This King has the appearance of a Bantam surrounded by full sized cockerels," Alan Dent remarked) and lack of voice were the common criticisms of his performance, on the one hand:

" In a performance of such majestic humanity, and simple authority that the falterings of a disjointed first act are soon forgotten," wrote Mr. Brian Harvey, " this young actor brings to the part a maturity and a singleness of mind

80

which give the production a quality of inward peace amid the cruelty of its scenes of war. Rhetorically, in the manner of other Harrys, it cannot perhaps rank as a great performance but imaginatively it is a thing of beauty."

And the critic in *Truth*:

"At present the full range of Henry is not within his grasp. His ringing voice, in the angry passages as well as in the lyrical heroics, lacks, as yet, the modulations of mature judgement; his variations of spoken pace suggest the breaking of monotony rather than the dictates of feelings. The trumpet tones before Harfleur probably suffer because they are spoken at the side of the hampering lock gate permanent set, but the performance begins in a key of excitement too highly pitched and hard to maintain. Nevertheless, it has much quiet humour and scorn, and the incognito mingling with the soldiery is beautifully done."

The critic in *The Times*, although he was one of those who had best caught the director's intentions throughout the series, was unconvinced by the performance:

"Mr. Richard Burton, conforming to the general design, has played Prince Hal as an Heir Apparent coolly awaiting his hour. But now that the hour has struck Mr. Burton is not quite able to make good Shakespeare's conception of the ideal King. He is effective enough in the rough exchanges with his Captains and soldiers, but his voice is scarcely equal to the rhetorical splendour of the patriotic parades and the soliloquies on Kingship, these are delivered on one note and lose importance. Accordingly, the story of a small and dauntless army which overcomes at odds of five to one an arrogant and morally debilitated enemy loses some of its natural excitement."

Mr. Ivor Brown in *The Observer* came out strongly in

opposition to these views about the part and its performance:

" This rapidly and justly arrived actor, was not chosen, obviously, for bravura qualities. He lacks the stature, the gait and trumpet note for greasepaint heroics . . . And so you may say he is not the Harry of Harfleur and Agincourt because he does not set the Avon on fire. But why not re-read the play before deciding so?"

And Mr. Brown proceeds to suggest that Henry V is not really " a strong-willed self-reliant man " but one who is egged into his war of aggression by the Church and by consideration of policy:

" These facts have been obscured," Mr. Brown continues, " because Shakespeare clapped on to the King's part a little — not a great deal — of battle rhetoric so intoxicating that few can think soberly of anything else in the character. (The Crispin Day speech is not rhetoric for a mass meeting of his men, but a colloquy with a few commanders and a briefing of them for their talks with the troops). Chorus, too, if the glorious lines are properly projected, sounds all the drums of romance. So theatrical tradition and public relish have seized on the vocalist of the battle cry and forgotten the " sudden student," the shrewd thinker, and the good pleader . . . So Richard Burton's performance, being true to what Shakespeare wrote and a clever continuance of his two earlier performances as the Prince, may disappoint those who are looking for the Lewis Waller of the 1950's whom, I grant, it would be very nice to discover. But I found his rendering of Henry faithful to Shakespeare's text and most intelligently spoken. This is a human, believable King, if not a soloist ' obliging ' on the clarion."

Though there were a number of dissentients, on the whole Mr. Quayle's production of this play did not please as much as the others, though without doubt, as so often happens, the first night performance did not give a fair picture. The critic in *The Times*, who had been so impressed with the earlier plays said of this one:

> "The rough figure of this production seems to run to detail. It is difficult to see the wood for the trees. We come away with no very vivid impressions of the play's outline and find that we have collected instead a number of minor unco-ordinated impressions.
>
> We remember, for instance, Mr. Hugh Griffith amusingly overdoing the Archbishop's political unscrupulousness when he is asked to pronounce on the rightness of the King's French claim; the suavity of Mr. Alan Badel as the elegantly boastful Dauphin, Miss Rosalind Atkinson's description of Falstaff's death; the larger-than-life Pistol of Mr. Richard Wordsworth; and some of the fighting at Agincourt, though since it is set against the permanent timber structure which has served the three histories of the Lancastrian revolution, that is remembered as having taken place on the quarter deck of a ship. These and similar scenes stand out; but it cannot be said that in the production as a whole Mr. Anthony Quayle has succeeded in bringing the three histories to a significant climax . . . Nor do the dusky banners and dim heraldic coats of Miss Tanya Moiseiwitsch do much to give the martial imagination the fillip it requires; they accord well with the dull permanent setting and that is their chief merit."

Mr. J. C. Trewin appears to have had the same experience of remembering the detail more clearly than the whole. In *The Sketch* he writes of his complaint about the production generally:

> "It has much superficial animation. The banners wave.

83

But at the premier I was not often moved, and then, as a rule, by small things; by Barbara Jefford's speaking of a few quite unremarkable lines for the Queen of France; by Duncan Lamont's heavy acceptance of defeat as Montjoy the Herald, ' The days is yours '; by the deep voice of Peter William's Exeter; and by Michael Gwynn as the mad Charles VI when he called the muster role of the French nobility, so often cut. But Mr. Gwynn overplays some of the King's scenes. The performance I shall remember most is Alan Badel's silken-insolent Dauphin, a fellow of dangerous quietness."

Mr. Phillip Hope-Wallace in *Time and Tide* was also rather critical:

"The comic characters are not as compact a group as they ought to be, but Pistol and Fluellen coalesce well in the end, when Richard Wordsworth and Robert Hardy have blossomed out in their full colours; Michael Gwynn's King Charles is a neurotic, jumpy, skull-faced man, whose weaknesses are enough to demoralise the whole court and army of France, and Alan Badel's Dauphin is not conceived as a strong enough man to exercise much counterbalancing effect. This means an establishment of feeling too early in the play that the French have no chance in the battles, whereas by Agincourt it should be clear that the English are the ones who are likely to be out-fought. It is a matter of production, just as Duncan Lamont's Montjoy by faltering entrances is made to appear much less important a character than he ought to be.

In fact the whole tone of the production — admirable though it is by the highest repertory standards — is inclined to make *Henry V* seem less important than it really is. The virtues of the production are steadiness, clear design, sufficient pace to avoid dullness most of the time and admirably clear speech. Its fault is that all these virtues have a somewhat negative total."

Comparison with the Old Vic's Festival production of the same play — in which Mr. Alec Clunes's fine voice dominated in the more conventional interpretation — could hardly be avoided and was not always to Stratford's advantage. Mr. Eric Keown in *Punch* wrote:

" The last of the plays does not rise to its full splendour of poetry and action. We have lately seen it done by the Old Vic almost perfectly to my mind, and Mr. Anthony Quayle's production compares unfavourably with that of the Waterloo Road. The edges are blurred; some of the finest poetry thrown away; the action is constricted and lacks sweep and contrast; and in the end we are left too conscious of the excellence of a few minor characters."

But this view was not universal. *The Manchester Guardian* critic writes:

" The first two thirds of this production, though a little too noisy to begin with, are a fine rounding off of the historical cycle. If Mr. Quayle can be considered as a conductor there are times when he does not seem sure whether it is a brass band or a military one that he is controlling. There are brazen notes alternated with more quietly harmonious woodwind passages. There are bannered moments and mannered ones, but the sum is a substantial sure-footed production . . . The nobles and the court surround their King with robust performance and the three traitors are more than usually creditable.

The ' continuity ' is in Michael Redgrave's hand as chorus. He is explosive at first, but soon conveys his own enthusiasmed excitement to the audience. The production

85

owes a great deal to him and to Tanya Moiseiwitsch whose
' unworthy scaffold ' proves an admirable foundation for
the play. It has served the whole historical cycle and in
Henry V supports the action and accelerates it. The stage
becomes Southampton by the draping of a few hemp ladders,
Harfleur by the dragging in of cannon, and the Court of
France by breaking out into ribbons and thrones. . . This is
not a great production because in spite of the King's solid
virtues and the vigour of Chorus it lacks a great performance.
But it is a well integrated production with only a few dull
passages; and on the whole a triumph of the ingenuity
which is the life of any repertory theatre."

Mr. Ivor Brown liked the production no less than Mr.
Richard Burton's interpretation of the King:

" The production, by Mr. Anthony Quayle has his usual
nice mixture of subtlety and vigour. It has also, as always
now at Stratford, a rich diversity in the minor roles. It is
not a play for the actress, but Hazel Penwarden is a pretty
Katherine. Raymond Westwell, as Williams, is a perfect
piece of plain blunt soldiery. Michael Bates and William
Squire could not be bettered as Bardolph and Nym . . .
Richard Wordsworth cleverly makes Pistol as little tiresome
as possible. Alan Badel and Michael Gwynn enliven the
arrogant and craven aspects of the French court, Hugh
Griffith is vividly the Canterbury fox."

Mr. Michael Redgrave's Chorus was sometimes criticised
(as in *The Times*) as coming " perilously near to tearing a
passion to tatters." Mr. Darlington in *The Daily Telegraph*
excuses this:

" Michael Redgrave as Chorus comes on and lashes
himself to a fine frenzy; and while at the time one feels that
Mr. Redgrave is perhaps overdoing it, afterwards one

realises that he has given the play a valuable flying start."

And Mr. Ivor Brown says of the performance that:

" It attacks the audience with a welcome, uninhibited relish of the poetry."

Once again the accidents of first night production rather told against the reception. Coming to it later in the season, I should have echoed Mr. Ivor Brown's " mixture of sublety and vigour." But I quite see how Mr. Burton's version of the King, consistent though it was with the whole design, may have left with others that slightly unsatisfying feeling of having been robbed of a climax.

CONCLUSION

ONE QUESTION about this most interesting presentation still remains: whether or not it supports the view that these four plays were originally designed by Shakespeare as one great play in four parts. I am not sufficiently expert in Shakespearian scholarship to be able to rehearse the arguments. I can only give my personal impression which is that, interesting and rewarding as the presentation in cycle is, it does not convince me that the plays were so designed. *Richard II*, even granted the additional interest which this presentation gives to its first two acts, yet still seems to me essentially a different kind of play, differently conceived from the other three, a play which, if it began as a chronicle, ended as something different. Then again *Henry IV* Part II seems to me so much weaker than Part I that it reminds one of those sequels which an author often mistakenly writes when a book of his has endeared itself to the public. This suggests to me the most probable way in which the plays came to be written in the condition of Elizabethan playwriting, namely that they *happened* one after the other. The success of *Richard II* suggest the idea of writing another historical play, but in the second play Shakespeare developed a better chronical method. Part II was the response to the public's demand for " More!", particularly more of Falstaff. While *Henry V* reflects a different demand from the audience, a demand which the poet had now developed a technique for meeting.

Whether this conjecture is true or not, in any case the rewards of this method of presentation are as I hope I have shown immense.

As a general summing up of this remarkable season I should like to give a long extract from the article by Mr. Robert Speaight in *The Tablet* of 8th September, 1951. Coming from a distinguished actor and producer, Mr. Speaight's tribute is all the more impressive:

" It is now possible to say that Shakespeare is better performed at Stratford than anywhere in the world, and a large share of the credit for this must go to Mr. Anthony Quayle, the present director of the Memorial Theatre. Mr. Quayle has the double merit of freshness and fidelity. He knows that each play must be studied anew, that it is not enough to repeat what has been done before, even if it has been done well; but he knows, too, that here the only true originality is in discovering what Shakespeare meant and in faithfully recording it. There is no point in an imaginative vision unless it is prepared to look at Shakespeare straight; and in the modern theatre the essential truth of the plays has too often been sacrificed to a producer's *parti pris*. (We had an example of this last year in Mr. Guthrie's cynical treatment of *Henry VIII*) and so the ambitious project of presenting Shakespeare's four histories as four closely-woven parts of a single drama would have failed utterly if Mr. Quayle and his assistants had approached their task in a spirit of wilfulness and condescension; if

88

they had started work with their minds made up instead of allowing Shakespeare to make them up for them.

These plays have always stood more or less successfully on their own feet, but when you see them played by the same actors on successive evenings they do not merely add up — they multiply. Mr. Quayle's conception of the tetralogy is brilliantly realised in terms of theatre; to attend these plays on successive nights is a unique and gathering excitement. Mr. Redgrave's Richard is perfectly felt and understood. Bolingbroke, instead of being three not-quite-star parts in three separate plays, becomes a great tragic protagonist, and Mr. Harry Andrews plays him magnificently, with a sick mind and a strong physique, restless and dominating to the end. So far, given artists of this calibre, was not, perhaps, so difficult, but there remained the problem of Prince Hal and Henry V. It is rarely possible to believe that these are one and the same person; Prince Hal is played by the juvenile lead and Henry V by the star — and that is about all there is to it. Yet the events of *Henry V* follow immediately on those of *Henry IV* Part II; if the young King who rejects Falstaff is not the same man who is going presently to challenge the French at Agincourt, Shakespeare has failed in his design. Mr. Quayle was therefore bound to find an actor who could develop plausibly from Eastcheap and Gadshill to Southampton and Harfleur; and in Mr. Richard Burton he has found him. This performance, like Mr. Redgrave's crazy Northumbrian Hotspur, is a genuine and justified surprise . . .

It is one consequence of treating the plays in this way that the problem of Falstaff disappears; or rather the audience's problem is the same as Shakespeare's — how best to get rid of him. His comic stature is in no way reduced, but we see him for what he is — a gigantic excrescence on the surface of the plays, the sign of Shakespeare's creative genius, the symbol of a genial and quite intolerable anarchy . . . By the time ' Harry has succeeded Harry ' we have had enough of him. He and his companions have served their dramatic purpose which was to show us the ' other England ' of slum and shire — the England that Henry was to govern and which, in order to govern, he had in some measure to know. But Shakespeare's purposes, like those of any great dramatist are generally more than dramatic, and these other purposes Falstaff super-abundantly fulfilled. Nevertheless, it is high time for him to go . . .

Mr. Burton not only takes the callousness out of Hal but he takes the chauvinism out of Harry. We who have watched the ravages of civil war through the two parts of *Henry IV* are ready to appreciate Bolingbroke's advice to " busy giddy minds with foreign quarrels." . . . Mr. Quayle has provided his actors with an Elizabethan setting, a triumph of ingenuity and good sense. This serves, with rapid and skilful adaptations, for court and countryside, tent and tavern. It allows the plays to flow practically uncut, with their natural rhythm. It gives to the actors not a decor which may easily become a distracton, but an architecture in which they may live and move and have their being. Against it Miss Moiseiwitsch's magnificent costumes sweep and glow . . . In sum, a very remarkable achievement, with rich rewards for the playgoer, new light for the student, and ripe instruction for anyone concerned with the management of the common weal."

Productions

KING RICHARD THE SECOND

BY ANTHONY QUAYLE

KING HENRY IV, Part I

BY ANTHONY QUAYLE

AND JOHN KIDD

KING HENRY IV, Part II

BY MICHAEL REDGRAVE

KING HENRY V

BY ANTHONY QUAYLE

★

Sets and Costumes designed by

TANYA MOISEIWITSCH

AND ALIX STONE

★

Music composed by

LESLIE BRIDGEWATER

★

Production Manager: PATRICK DONNELL

KING RICHARD THE SECOND

KING RICHARD the Second .. .. MICHAEL REDGRAVE
JOHN OF GAUNT, Duke of Lancaster, *uncle to the King* HUGH GRIFFITH
HENRY BOLINGBROKE, Duke of Hereford, *son to Gaunt*
HARRY ANDREWS
THOMAS MOWBRAY, Duke of Norfolk .. WILLIAM FOX
DUCHESS OF GLOUCESTER .. .. ROSALIND ATKINSON
DUKE OF SURREY .. .. JACK GWILLIM
DUKE OF AUMERLE, *son to the Duke of York* BASIL HOSKINS
HERALD TO BOLINGBROKE .. .. .. LEO CICERI
HERALD TO MOWBRAY .. .. RONALD HINES
SIR HENRY GREEN ⎱ *friends* ⎰ .. MICHAEL MEACHAM
SIR JOHN BUSHY ⎰ *to the* ⎱ .. RICHARD WORDSWORTH
SIR WILLIAM BAGOT ⎰ *King* ⎱ .. .. PETER JACKSON
EDMUND LANGLEY, Duke of York, *uncle to the King*
MICHAEL GWYNN
QUEEN to King Richard .. .. .. HEATHER STANNARD
EARL OF NORTHUMBERLAND .. .. ALEXANDER GAUGE
LORD ROSS .. .. PHILIP MORANT
LORD WILLOUGHBY .. .. MICHAEL BATES
SERVANT TO YORK .. .. .. GEOFFREY BAYLDON
HENRY PERCY, surnamed HOTSPUR, *son to Northumberland*
ROBERT HARDY
LORD BERKELEY .. .. BRENDON BARRY
EARL OF SALISBURY .. .. .. PETER NORRIS
CAPTAIN OF A BAND OF WELSHMEN .. RAYMOND WESTWELL
BISHOP OF CARLISLE .. .. DUNCAN LAMONT
SIR STEPHEN SCROOP .. .. PETER WILLIAMS
⎰ MARJORIE STEEL
LADIES ATTENDING ON THE QUEEN ⎱ RACHEL ROBERTS
⎰ HAZEL PENWARDEN
FIRST GARDENER .. .. GODFREY BOND
SECOND GARDENER .. .. .. EDWARD ATIENZA
LORD FITZWATER .. .. PETER HALLIDAY
ABBOT OF WESTMINSTER .. .. .. PETER HENCHIE
DUCHESS OF YORK .. .. .. JOAN MACARTHUR
SIR PIERCE of Exton .. .. WILLIAM SQUIRE
GROOM .. .. JOHN GAY
KEEPER .. .. REGINALD MARSH

Lords, Soldiers and Attendants: MICHAEL FERREY, KEITH FAULKNER, IAN BANNEN, JOHN FOSTER, TIMOTHY HARLEY, RALPH HALLETT, MICHAEL HAYES, JAMES MOSS, DAVID ORR, CLIFFORD PARRISH, ALAN TOWNSEND, KENNETH WYNNE.

93

KING HENRY IV
PART I

KING HENRY IV		HARRY ANDREWS
HENRY, Prince of Wales ⎞ *Sons to the* ⎰		RICHARD BURTON
JOHN of Lancaster ⎰ *King* ⎱		.. JOHN GAY
EARL OF WESTMORELAND ⎞ *Friends to* ⎰		.. JACK GWILLIM
SIR WALTER BLUNT ⎰ *the King* ⎱		RAYMOND WESTWELL
THOMAS PERCY, Earl of Worcester ..		DUNCAN LAMONT
HENRY PERCY, Earl of Northumberland		ALEXANDER GAUGE
HENRY PERCY, surnamed HOTSPUR, *his son*		MICHAEL REDGRAVE
EDMUND MORTIMER, Earl of March ..		.. PETER WILLIAMS
OWEN GLENDOWER		.. HUGH GRIFFITH
ARCHIBALD, Earl of Douglas		.. PHILIP MORANT
SIR RICHARD VERNON		.. WILLIAM FOX
RICHARD SCROOP, Archbishop of York..		.. ROBERT HARDY
SIR MICHAEL, *a friend to the Archbishop of York*		MICHAEL FERREY
SIR JOHN FALSTAFF		ANTHONY QUAYLE
POINS		.. ALAN BADEL
BARDOLPH		.. MICHAEL BATES
PETO		PETER HALLIDAY
GADSHILL		EDWARD ATIENZA
FRANCIS, *a drawer*		MICHAEL MORGAN
CHAMBERLAIN		.. GODFREY BOND
FIRST CARRIER		.. RONALD HINES
SECOND CARRIER		REGINALD MARSH
FIRST TRAVELLER		KENNETH WYNNE
SECOND TRAVELLER		.. ROBERT HARDY
VINTNER		.. MICHAEL FERREY
SHERIFF		.. PETER HENCHIE
SERVANT TO HOTSPUR		DAVID ORR

MISTRESS QUICKLY, *hostess of a tavern in Eastcheap*

ROSALIND ATKINSON

LADY PERCY, *wife to Hotspur and sister to Mortimer*

BARBARA JEFFORD

LADY MORTIMER, *daughter to Glendower and wife to Mortimer*

SYBIL WILLIAMS

Lords, Soldiers, Citizens, Servants: HAZEL PENWARDEN, JOAN MAC-ARTHUR, RACHEL ROBERTS, IAN BANNEN, BRENDON BARRY, LEO CICERI, JOHN FOSTER, RALPH HALLETT, MICHAEL HAYES, BASIL HOSKINS, PETER JACKSON, MICHAEL MEACHAM, JAMES MOSS, CLIFFORD PARRISH, ALAN TOWNSEND, KEITH FAULKNER, ROBERT SANDFORD.

KING HENRY IV
PART II

RUMOUR	.. WILLIAM SQUIRE
KING HENRY the Fourth	.. HARRY ANDREWS
HENRY, Prince of Wales	RICHARD BURTON
THOMAS, Duke of Clarence *his*	BRENDON BARRY
PRINCE JOHN OF LANCASTER *sons*	.. JOHN GAY
PRINCE HUMPHREY OF GLOSTER	MICHAEL MEACHAM
EARL OF WARWICK..	.. PETER JACKSON
EARL OF WESTMORELAND	.. JACK GWILLIM
EARL OF SURREY *of the*	MICHAEL FERREY
LORD CHIEF-JUSTICE *King's*	MICHAEL GWYNN
GOWER *party*	REGINALD MARSH
HARCOURT	.. BASIL HOSKINS
EARL OF NORTHUMBERLAND	ALEXANDER GAUGE
SCROOP, Archbishop of York *against*	.. ROBERT HARDY
LORD MOWBRAY *the*	.. PETER WILLIAMS
LORD HASTINGS *King*	.. PETER NORRIS
SIR JOHN COLEVILE	.. PHILIP MORANT
PORTER	.. LEO CICERI
TRAVERS *retainers of*	.. PETER HALLIDAY
MORTON *Northumberland*	RAYMOND WESTWELL
SIR JOHN FALSTAFF	ANTHONY QUAYLE
HIS PAGE	.. KEITH FAULKNER
BARDOLPH	.. MICHAEL BATES
POINS	.. ALAN BADEL
PISTOL	.. RICHARD WORDSWORTH
PETO	.. PETER HALLIDAY
FRANCIS, *a drawer*	.. TIMOTHY HARLEY
ANOTHER DRAWER	.. BRENDON BARRY
FANG *Sheriff's*	EDWARD ATIENZA
SNARE *Officers*	.. PETER HENCHIE
SHALLOW *Country*	.. ALAN BADEL
SILENCE *Justices*	WILLIAM SQUIRE
DAVY, *servant to Shallow*	ALEXANDER GAUGE
MOULDY	.. KENNETH WYNNE
SHADOW	:: GODFREY BOND
WART *Recruits*	EDWARD ATIENZA
FEEBLE	GEOFFREY BAYLDON
BULLCALF	.. RONALD HINES
LADY NORTHUMBERLAND	JOAN MACARTHUR
LADY PERCY	.. BARBARA JEFFORD
MISTRESS QUICKLY, *hostess of a tavern in Eastcheap*	ROSALIND ATKINSON
DOLL TEARSHEET	HEATHER STANNARD

Lords, Soldiers, Citizens and Attendants: RACHEL ROBERTS, MARJORIE STEEL, SYBIL WILLIAMS, IAN BANNEN, JOHN FOSTER, RALPH HALLETT, MICHAEL HAYES, JAMES MOSS, DAVID ORR, CLIFFORD PARRISH, ROBERT SANDFORD, ALAN TOWNSEND.

95

KING HENRY V

CHORUS	MICHAEL REDGRAVE*
ARCHBISHOP OF CANTERBURY ..	.. HUGH GRIFFITH
BISHOP OF ELY	EDWARD ATIENZA
KING HENRY the Fifth	RICHARD BURTON
DUKE OF GLOUCESTER ⎱ brothers to ⎰	MICHAEL MEACHAM
DUKE OF BEDFORD ⎰ the King ⎱ ..	JOHN GAY
DUKE OF EXETER, uncle to the King ..	PETER WILLIAMS
DUKE OF YORK, cousin to the King ..	.. BASIL HOSKINS
EARL OF WESTMORELAND	JACK GWILLIM
EARL OF WARWICK	PETER JACKSON
EARL OF SALISBURY	.. MICHAEL FERREY
EARL OF CAMBRIDGE	RAYMOND WESTWELL
LORD SCROOP of Masham	.. BRENDON BARRY
SIR THOMAS GREY	.. RALPH HALLETT
SIR THOMAS ERPINGHAM	.. GODFREY BOND
GOWER .. .. ⎱ ⎰	REGINALD MARSH
FLUELLEN .. ⎱ Officers in ⎰	.. ROBERT HARDY
MACMORRIS .. ⎰ King Henry's Army ⎱	GEOFFREY BAYLDON
JAMY .. .. ⎰ ⎱	.. DAVID ORR
PISTOL	..RICHARD WORDSWORTH*
BARDOLPH	.. MICHAEL BATES
NYM	.. WILLIAM SQUIRE
HOSTESS, formerly MISTRESS QUICKLY	ROSALIND ATKINSON
FRANCIS	TIMOTHY HARLEY
WILLIAMS .. ⎱ Soldiers in ⎰	RAYMOND WESTWELL
BATES .. .. ⎰ King Henry's Army ⎱	.. MICHAEL BATES
COURT .. .. ⎰ ⎱	.. RONALD HINES
ENGLISH HERALD	.. JOHN FOSTER
CHARLES the Sixth, King of France ..	MICHAEL GWYNN
LEWIS, the Dauphin	.. ALAN BADEL
DUKE OF ORLEANS	.. PHILIP MORANT
DUKE OF BOURBON	RONALD HINES
THE CONSTABLE OF FRANCE	WILLIAM FOX
LORD GRANDPRÉ	.. WILLIAM SQUIRE
LORD RAMBURES	ALAN TOWNSEND
MONTJOY, the French Herald	.. DUNCAN LAMONT
GOVERNOR OF HARFLEUR	PETER HENCHIE
FIRST FRENCH MESSENGER	.. BRENDON BARRY
SECOND FRENCH MESSENGER	PETER HALLIDAY
A FRENCH SOLDIER	..KENNETH WYNNE
DUKE OF BURGUNDY	PETER NORRIS
ISABEL, Queen of France	BARBARA JEFFORD
KATHERINE, daughter to Charles and Isabel	HAZEL PENWARDEN
ALICE, a lady attending on her	ROSALIND ATKINSON

Ladies-in-Waiting, Soldiers, Sailors, Citizens, Servants: JOAN MACARTHUR,
RACHEL ROBERTS, MARJORIE STEEL, SYBIL WILLIAMS, IAN BANNEN, LEO
CICERI, MICHAEL HAYES, JAMES MOSS, CLIFFORD PARRISH, KEITH
FAULKNER, ROBERT SANDFORD.

* For the later weeks of the season the part of *Chorus* was played by
WILLIAM SQUIRE and the part of *Pistol* by ROBERT EDDISON.